March 16, 1993

God bless you and yours.

Think of your 8:30 A.M. Tuesday prayer partners; <u>often</u>.

We love you.

Lormie Wascon

Ruby Cabler

Opal Rae Wild

Ruth P. Keen

Dorothy Gunn

Layman's Bible Book Commentary
Isaiah

LAYMAN'S BIBLE BOOK COMMENTARY

ISAIAH
VOLUME 10

Trent C. Butler

BROADMAN PRESS
Nashville, Tennessee

© Copyright 1982 • Broadman Press.

All rights reserved.

4211-80

ISBN: 0-8054-1180-1

Dewey Decimal Classification: 224.1

Subject Heading: BIBLE. O.T. ISAIAH

Library of Congress Catalog Card Number: 80-68890

Printed in the United States of America

Foreword

The *Layman's Bible Book Commentary* in twenty-four volumes was planned as a practical exposition of the whole Bible for lay readers and students. It is based on the conviction that the Bible speaks to every generation of believers but needs occasional reinterpretation in the light of changing language and modern experience. Following the guidance of God's Spirit, the believer finds in it the authoritative word for faith and life.

To meet the needs of lay readers, the *Commentary* is written in a popular style, and each Bible book is clearly outlined to reveal its major emphases. Although the writers are competent scholars and reverent interpreters, they have avoided critical problems and the use of original languages except where they were essential for explaining the text. They recognize the variety of literary forms in the Bible, but they have not followed documentary trails or become preoccupied with literary concerns. Their primary purpose was to show what each Bible book meant for its time and what it says to our own generation.

The Revised Standard Version of the Bible is the basic text of the *Commentary*, but writers were free to use other translations to clarify an occasional passage or sharpen its effect. To provide as much interpretation as possible in such concise books, the Bible text was not printed along with the comment.

Of the twenty-four volumes of the *Commentary*, fourteen deal with Old Testament books and ten with those in the New Testament. The volumes range in pages from 140 to 168. Four major books in the Old Testament and five in the New are treated in one volume each. Others appear in various combinations. Although the allotted space varies, each Bible book is treated as a whole to reveal its basic message with some passages getting special attention. Whatever plan of Bible study the reader may follow, this *Commentary* will be a valuable companion.

Despite the best-seller reputation of the Bible, the average survey of Bible knowledge reveals a good deal of ignorance about it and its primary meaning. Many adult church members seem to think that its study is intended for children and preachers. But some of the newer translations have been making the Bible more readable for all ages. Bible study has branched out from Sunday into other days of the week, and into neighborhoods rather than just in churches. This *Commentary* wants to meet the growing need for insight into all that the Bible has to say about God and his world and about Christ and his fellowship.

BROADMAN PRESS

Contents

ISAIAH

ISAIAH

Introduction

Isaiah ushers us into the wonder-filled world of the prophets. Heroic visions race through our minds at the mention of the word *prophets*. But what is the job description of a prophet? What common factors bind Samuel and Malachi, Elisha and Amos, Isaiah and Obadiah? Why does the ministry of an Elijah produce stories in Kings, while Amos' results in a collection of his sermons?

A student of the Bible must face such questions before he can hope to understand biblical prophecy. We can give only brief hints for reflection here by discussing prophetic culture, community, calling, context, content, collection, and canonization.

The Prophetic Culture

The culture in which prophecy was at home extended far beyond Israel, appearing in various forms in Egypt, Babylon, Syria, and Phoenicia. Prophets bringing words to kings appeared in Mari, a Syrian town on the Euphrates River, seven hundred years before Saul or David. The Bible records that other gods had their prophets (1 Kings 18:19-20; 2 Kings 10:19; Jer. 29:9). Prophecy was not static but changed as the culture changed.

The Prophetic Community

Such change is seen in the prophetic community. For Samuel the prophetic community included a group of prophets living together at the place of worship (1 Sam. 10:5). At other times, prophets lived at the king's court (1 Kings 1; 18; 22). Some simply followed prophetic leaders (2 Kings 4:1; 9:1; compare Isa. 8:16). Prophetic groups could be large (1 Kings 18:4; 22:6), but prophets could feel lonely and isolated (1 Kings 19:10; Jer. 15:17). They even faced prophetic competition (1 Kings 22:24; Jer. 27—28). At times they faced public contempt for their unusual conduct (1 Sam. 10:6; 19:24; 2 Kings 2:23-25; Isa. 20:1-5; Hos. 1; Ezek. 4). These changing prophetic communities performed an important task for God's people. They preserved the accounts and sermons of the prophets.

The Prophetic Calling

At the center of these communities stood the prophetic calling! This was a very personal experience. Each was different—coming in visions (Isa. 6), dreams (1 Sam. 2), or in a sense of destination from birth (Jer. 1). Each brought a sense of inadequacy. Each brought a compulsion to preach. Each resulted in continuing experiences with God that brought new messages for new historical situations.

The Prophetic Context

The prophet can be understood only within the context of history. Prophets preached to Israel for at least seven hundred years, from the time of Deborah the prophetess (Judg. 4:4) to the time of Malachi or even later. Each faced different problems, different temptations, different needs. The same prophet saw drastic changes in his context, as we will see with Isaiah. Only new experiences with God could provide the needed word for the moment.

Not only the historical context changed. The social context changed as well. Samuel and Isaiah were closely related to the Temple (1 Sam. 2; Isa. 6). Amos and Jeremiah were forbidden to enter the Temple (Amos 7; Jer. 36:5). Ezekiel lived in exile, far removed from the Temple. Haggai and Zechariah sought to rebuild a destroyed Temple. Amos came from the south to preach to the north, while Hosea was a northerner preaching to his own people. The other prophets apparently preached in the Southern Kingdom. Many spoke directly to the king in private conversation (Isa. 7; 38; Jer. 22). We understand the preacher and his message better when we know when, where, and to whom he preached. Most prophetic words do not directly state where and when they were preached. It is the work of the commentator to help us find this information.

The Prophetic Content

Most importantly, we search for the content of prophetic preaching. Theologically, we claim that the words of the prophet are words of God. This is the starting point for any statement about prophetic preaching. Yet each prophet had his own vocabulary, his own themes, his own way of speaking. How do we interpret this?

At least three types of evidence crack the door just a bit for us to understand this awesome mystery and power of inspiration. First, the prophet could speak and identify with his audience because of his own deeply personal experiences. The word of God was based on the agonizing marriage experience of Hosea, the life-changing encounter with the holy God by Isaiah, the fantastic visions of Ezekiel, the impatient waiting on the watchman's stand by Habakkuk, and the painful personal struggle with God by Jeremiah. God showed his spokesmen how to formulate into language their deeply personal experiences.

God gave his prophets yet another tool, the basic language formulas which alerted the audience to the moods and scenes the prophet was setting. An understanding of such language formulas helps us understand the prophetic books. We will look briefly at the most obvious ones.

The *prophecy of disaster* begins with a call to listen as in Isaiah 1:10 or 7:13. It is followed by an accusation listing the sins of the audience as in Isaiah 1:11-12; 7:13*b*. The conclusion is the prediction of disaster beginning "Therefore, thus says the Lord" (see 1:24-25). When the audience heard this "Therefore," they knew bad news was coming.

The *prophetic woe oracle* was borrowed from Israel's funeral ceremonies. First, the prophet cried out "Woe," the word of sorrow and grief. This showed the emotional empathy of the prophet for his people. Then the prophet listed the sins of the people, followed by the announcement of judgment. Isaiah 5:8-10 is a good example.

The prophet often imitated a *courtroom trial*. He summoned witnesses to court (1:2; 5:3), reported the lawyer's questioning of defendant and witnesses (5:4), and announced the verdict and sentence (5:5-6).

The prophet borrowed language for his *oracle of salvation* from the Temple priests, whose job it was to assure the worshiper who came to the Temple in time of trouble. The oracle of salvation begins, "Do not fear." It promised God's help and described the result of such help (Isa. 7:4-7).

These were the major linguistic tools of the prophetic trade, tools which the prophets borrowed from the courtroom, the funeral parlor, and the Temple, among other places. Such tools help us today as we try to separate individual prophetic sermons from one another. They help us in our search for the social context of the prophet and in our attempts to recreate the mood of the congregation as the prophet preached. They alert us to the fact that the prophets borrowed their language from all areas of daily life, so that we must be alert to discover new forms of speech which the prophets transformed for their own purposes.

The prophets had yet another tool given them as they preached God's word to his people. This was the *religious tradition of Israel*. The prophets did not speak in a vacuum. They spoke to people who worshiped the creator God who had led Israel's fathers from Mesopotamia into the land of Canaan then into Egypt and back out again in the Exodus. Their God had directed a murmuring people through the wilderness to Sinai, given them the law, and led them on through the wilderness to the Promised Land. God's history did not end there. Kingship was requested and accepted, a Temple was built, and Temple worship practices developed. All of these gave new language which the prophets used to explain God's new purposes to the audiences. We can learn much if we carefully observe which traditions the particular prophet used and how he used old language to proclaim the new Word of God in the new historical context.

The Prophetic Collection

The prophetic content could have died in its own historical context without God's intervention. After all, the writing prophets generally opposed the established political and religious institutions. It is most unlikely that the kings of Israel and Judah or the priests of the Jerusalem Temple gladly welcomed the prophets and carefully preserved their words. Instead, many of the kings chose to disregard the prophets (Isa. 7), and one even burned a prophet's words (Jer. 36). The priests told the prophets to go home and quit preaching (Amos 7) or beat them and put them in prison (Jer. 20:1-2). Even had the preaching found its way into the Temple or court archives, the destruction of Jerusalem in 587 BC might have destroyed their preaching forever.

As God inspired the prophet in his preaching, he also inspired the prophetic community to recognize the authority and truth of the prophetic word even when the political and religious powers rejected the prophet and tried to destroy his words. Small bands of faithful prophetic disciples (Isa. 8; Jer. 36:4) collected the master's preaching and committed it to writing. Such writings did not lie dormant for the four hundred or so years from Isaiah until Malachi waiting for the prophetic canon to be complete. No! Preservation included proclamation. The disciples of the prophets preached and interpreted the prophet's words, handing them down to new generations of faithful followers. The prophetic word was used by God to speak not simply to one generation but to continuing generations of the people of God. These unknown inspired disciples of the prophets preserved God's Word so that it could resound through the ages.

The Prophetic Canonization

Such gradual collection of the prophetic word led to one final amazing step. The word rejected so soundly by Israel's political and religious institutions proved itself true (note Deut. 13:1-5; 18:15-22; 1 Kings 22:28; Jer. 28; 42:1-7). The small group of faithful followers preached the words of the prophets and proved to society-at-large that the prophets had indeed spoken the word of God. The canonization of Scripture began. Prophetic preaching from many prophets over many centuries was collected.

This was not a simple process, however. The community did not remain in one spot. Political reality spread the Jewish community into Babylon, Egypt, Phoenicia, and many other parts of the globe. Translations of the Old Testament Scriptures were needed. The earliest Greek translation we know was probably completed in the third century before Christ. We call it the Septuagint. It is a Greek translation of the Hebrew Old Testament. It also shows us the earliest stage of the interpretation of the Hebrew Bible available for study.

The pathway to canonization was not easy and certain. It was uphill all the way, because people continued to ignore or reject God's prophetic messengers. Yet God led in every step to preserve his Word so his people could understand his ways with mankind. He called prophets in their culture, gave them his content for their context, and then raised up and protected for centuries a line of faithful followers to gather a collection of prophetic preaching and lift it finally to its rightfully-won place as canon for the people of God. From their hands we take up the canon, continue the task of interpreting and preserving it for our day, and then pass it on to the generation which God will raise up after us.

The Historical Context of Isaiah

This understanding of prophecy forces us to ask another major question. What was the historical context of Isaiah and of those who preserved his words? The answer is unexpectedly complex. Isaiah 6:1 tells us the prophet received his call in the year King Uzziah died. This can be dated only approximately between 747 and 736; say 740 BC for easy reference. Isaiah 45:1 names Cyrus as the agent used by God to deliver Judah from Exile. Cyrus founded the Persian empire and ruled from 559 to 530 BC. No prophet lived both under Uzziah and under Cyrus. How do we explain the data?

Two theories have been proposed. Both assume that God inspired the words of the Book of Isaiah. Either an eighth-century Isaiah knew names and events of history which took place two hundred years later, or the disciples of Isaiah continued to interpret his words for the following centuries and updated his message for their day under the guidance of God. The problem has been argued at least since the time of the Jewish rabbi Ibn Ezra, about 1167 AD.

The question centers around three types of data: the nature of the message, the type of traditional material used, and the historical context. The call of Isaiah emphasized the judgment brought by the prophet (ch. 6), while chapter 40 introduces a section dominated by "Comfort ye my people" (KJV). The traditions of God's election of Jerusalem, the Temple, and the king recur throughout chapters 1—39, while the traditions of Exodus, creation, wilderness, and conquest are the important elements in 40—66. The historical setting presupposed in the two sections is separated by over two hundred years of history.

Fortunately, the question of authorship is not the vital one. What is vital is the affirmation that God sought to direct the history of his people. Our task is to understand the historical situation addressed by the prophet and the reaction expected from the people of God in that situation. This we seek to determine as we examine the book. To do so, we will use the following outline of the history of Israel.

I. The Assyrian Period
    A. Tiglath-pileser III (745-727)
        1. Collects tribute from Menahem (742) of Israel and Rezin of Damascus (738).

      2. Israel and Damascus join in revolt and try to force Judah to participate by besieging Jerusalem in Syro-Ephraimitic War (734).

      3. Ahaz (735-715) of Judah summons Tiglath-pileser to help, bringing destruction of Damascus and reduction of Israel to small city-state around Samaria (732) with new king Hoshea (731-723) (2 Kings 16:5 to 17:1).

  B. Shalmaneser V (727-722) besieges Samaria (724-722), which was then captured either by him or by Sargon II.

  C. Sargon II (722-705)

      1. Subdues rebellions in Babylon, Hamath, Gaza, and Samaria, while collecting tribute from Judah (720). Egypt defeated for first time.

      2. Hezekiah (715-687) becomes king of Judah, bringing religious and political reforms (2 Kings 18).

      3. Ashdod revolt is put down (712).

      4. Babylon revolt fails (710).

  D. Sennacherib (705-681)

      1. Subdues rebels in Assyria and Babylon.

      2. Defeats Phoenicians, Philistines, Egyptians (701).

      3. Destroys most Judean cities and besieges Jerusalem (701), but has to retreat to Nineveh (2 Kings 18:13 to 19:37; Isa. 36—37).

      4. Manasseh begins reign as Judean king (687-642).

  E. Esarhaddon (680-669)

  F. Ashurbanipal (668-631) marks beginning of end of Assyrian power with major revolts in 642 a contributing factor to assassination of Ammon of Judah (642-640) and rise of independent Josiah (640-609) (2 Kings 22—23).

II. The Babylonian Period

  A. Nabopolassar (626-605)

      1. Fall of Asshur and fall of Nineveh (614-12) mark end of Assyrian empire.

      2. Josiah killed at Megiddo (609) by Egyptians (2 Kings 23:29-30), succeeded by Jehoahaz, then Jehoiachim (609-598).

  B. Nebuchadnezzar II (605-562)

      1. Defeats Pharaoh Necho of Egypt at Carchemish to gain control over Syria-Palestine (605).

      2. Invasion of Egypt fails (601), encouraging Judah's revolt.

3. Defeats Jerusalem (597), sends large numbers including Ezekiel and new king Jehoichin into Exile, and names Zedekiah (597-587) king (2 Kings 24:1-17).
4. Judean rebellions in 594, then 589, with Egyptian encouragement, led to final destruction of Jerusalem (587/586) (2 Kings 24).
5. Further exile of Jewish citizens in 582 (Jeremiah 52:30).

C. Amel-Marduk, Evil-merodach in KJV and RSV, (562-560) releases Jehoiachin from prison (2 Kings 25:27; Jeremiah 52:31).

D. Nabonidus (555-539) busies himself with travels and archaeology projects, so that much responsibility fell on his son and co-regent Belshazzar.

III. The Persian Period

A. Cyrus the Great (559-530)
1. Founds Persian empire (559).
2. Captures Babylon without resistance (539).
3. Issues edict (538) allowing Jews to return home (Ezra 1:1).
4. Work begins on Jerusalem Temple (538-537) (Ezra 3:6-8).

B. Cambyses (530-522) conquers Egypt (525).

C. Darius (522-486) led revolution.
1. Work on Temple begins anew under Zerubbabel, Joshua, Haggai, and Zechariah (520-518).
2. New Temple dedicated (515) (Ezra 6:15-18).
3. Darius loses battle of Marathon to Greeks (490).

Within this historical framework, we can understand each of the short sermons preserved in the Book of Isaiah. We will refer to this chart and to that on prophetic language to place each of the sermons in context.

Restoration Through Repentance
1:1 to 12:6

Doom dominates the content of Isaiah 1—12. This we expected from the prophet's commission to harden the hearts and blind the eyes of his people (ch. 6). The order and structure of the twelve chapters, however, show that disaster was not the last word. Light shone through the darkness. Great rays of hope brightened the stage at the climax of the section (9:2-7; 10:1 to 11:16), bringing forth the great hymn of thanksgiving in chapter 12. So despite all the dark moments, the theme of the opening section is restoration for a repentant remnant.

The Message in a Minute (1:1-31)

The faithful disciples who compiled the prophet's preaching were realists. They provided a quick summary which could be read in a minute. Sermons from different periods of Isaiah's ministry were joined to picture a courtroom trial against God's people.

Calling the Confused to Court (1:1-3)

About 740 BC, Summons to witness. (See the outline of history chart on pages 16-18 to understand the context of each of these notations throughout this volume.) A preface describes Isaiah's words as based on visions or dreams. The message itself begins by calling the universe to the jury box to hear God's accusation. The charge is blunt: God's people are dumber than beasts of burden, who at least know the hand that feeds them. God's people don't even know their heavenly Father. Israel shared this concept of God as Father with her neighbors and so used the concept cautiously. Here it refers to God as concerned for his children, whom he educates in vain.

Lamenting the Lost (1:4-9)

701 BC, Woe oracle. Not a stern, impassive judge, but a mourning father brought the accusation against the defendant Israel. The accusation is loaded with theological words. "Sinful" refers to breaking a personal relationship, not just a single law (Gen. 50:17). "Iniquity" is a life-style bent out of shape, crooked (Isa. 30:13). "Evildoers" are wicked in the most general and encompassing sense. "Deal corruptly" is a military term referring to destruction which eliminates the possibility for human well-being. Such action showed that the people had forsaken, rejected God. The sad fact was that the people were unaware of the consequences of their actions and attitudes. They thought they continued to be the people of God. The prophet had to reveal the reality to them. The personal relationship of mutual love and trust similar to that between parent and child had disappeared.

God is here called the "Holy One of Israel," a favorite term of Isaiah. Otherwise the phrase appears only in Jeremiah 50:29; 51:5; Psalm 71:22; 78:41; 89:19. The call experience of Isaiah (ch. 6) gave a new intensity of meaning to this description of God, who was totally pure in contrast to mankind's sinfulness. This holy God tried to argue sense into Israel's head, describing her desperate condition after the invasion of Sennacherib. Only God's grace had allowed them to escape the fate of Sodom and Gomorrah (Gen. 18—19). God had diagnosed Israel's pains, but Israel would not return to him for healing.

Reviving the Religious (1:10-17)

About 740 or 715 BC, Courtroom accusation, based on prophetic instruction. On a national holiday the prophet saw the herds of animals being brought for sacrifice, then stood up in his role of teacher. He identified the congregation with the ancient people from Sodom and Gomorrah. His listeners stood in stunned silence. Were they really Sodomites? The prophet followed with a question that seemed to be rather dumb in the setting of religious festival: Why are you sacrificing? They responded: Moses told us to; we've always done so! The prophet shocked them further: God says, in effect, "I'm full up to here; I can't stuff another bite down my throat!"

The prophet had a new teaching, a new law: no more offerings, no more festivals, no more prayers. Did Isaiah want to close the doors of the Temple? No! He wanted to set priorities straight. Worship must not shield people from God's claim upon their lives. Gifts cannot replace personal action. Ritual does not rectify. Sacrifice does not substitute for service. Justice must be provided for all people before the jury allows the Temple doors to open. Then ritual can be in response to the riches of God, our Redeemer.

Reasoning for Repentance (1:18-20)

705 BC, Prophetic call to repent. The judge did not pronounce the sentence. He laid a choice before the accused. The evidence was clear. The verdict: guilty. The divine judge offered one more chance, however, for a new start. Would Israel obey and prosper or remain rebellious and die?

Recycling the Righteous (1:21-26)

740 BC, Funeral lamentation and woe oracle. While the city was enjoying the height of prosperity, the prophet described the funeral of Jerusalem. He pictured the city as a bride who had forsaken her husband for the world's oldest profession. "Faithful" means strong and enduring, as well as loyal and believing. It represents the basic demand of Isaiah (7:9; 8:2; 22:23,25; 28:16; 33:16). Israel scorned strength for stealing and self-interest. Bribes became more important than belief. She rejected the requirements of verses 16-17,19. The Lord of hosts could not ignore this. In sorrowful anger the Mighty One moved.

Here are two ancient titles for Israel's God. The military designation "Lord of hosts" was connected to the ark of the covenant which had led Israel's armies to victory (1 Sam. 1:3,11; 4:4; 6:2). The name "Lord of Hosts" is used 62 times in Isaiah; 82 in Jeremiah; 53 in Zechariah; and 24 in Malachi—285 times in the Old Testament. "Mighty One of Israel" occurs only here, but the related term "Mighty One of Jacob" rings forth in Genesis 49:24; Isaiah 49:26; 60:16; Psalm 132:2,5. The mighty, divine general must put his hand to the smelter to recycle his rebellious people. Isaiah had hope for the nation, but only after he buried it.

Burning the Baal-Lovers (1:27-31)

Prophecy of disaster. The combination of hope and threat finds explicit interpretation. The question at issue is Zion, a word filled with theological importance. Zion was the southeastern hill of the city of Jerusalem (2 Sam. 5:7), where Solomon built the Temple. The term was then extended to designate all of Jerusalem as the holy city. Temple worshipers raised hymns of praise to the city (Pss. 46; 48; 76:1-3; 84; 87; 122; 132). It was God's "resting place for ever," which he chose (Ps. 132:14).

Isaiah dared disagree. He modified popular opinion. Zion had to be redeemed by God because she was sinful. Such redemption would bring human justice. This is biblical redemption—God's redemption of persons resulting in human justice on earth.

Here such justice was given an unusual interpretation. Justice produces embarrassment at improper religion. Israel's sin was the worship of the Canaanite Baal in holy trees and gardens. The divine Judge would ultimately pronounce his sentence—death by burning. With the judgment, there remained hope for those who repented (v. 27).

Deliverance and Doom in That Day (2:1 to 4:6)

The summary court trial of chapter one leads to a section with a new introduction (2:1) in which the day of God's action takes center stage. Again the major message is doom and darkness, but this is encased (2:2-4; 4:2-6) in glorious hope.

The Way to Warless Worship for the World (2:1-5)

701 BC, Oracle of salvation. Isaiah and his younger contemporary Micah have both used the same call to worship from the Jerusalem Temple to speak to God's people (see Mic. 4:1-5). Whereas the destruction of Jerusalem dominated chapter 1, her function as the center of world salvation introduces this section. We look to the "latter days" but still to world history with separate nations acting. Israel joined her Near Eastern neighbors in talking about the national Temple as the highest mountain on earth where the deity fights battles for his people (compare Pss. 46; 48).

As usual, the prophet took up the popular theology and subtly shifted the emphasis, shifting everything to the future. Only in the latter days would Zion occupy such an exalted position. God would no longer battle the nations. Jerusalem could no longer glory in the hope that nations would march to her with large gifts and tribute for her victorious king. The prophetic hope is that God's word will become the world's weapon. Military academies and weapons will vanish. The world's only war will be on poverty and hunger. The prophet knew only one way for this to happen. Thus he issued his own call to worship (v. 5). This worship is not limited to the Temple but shines forth in everyday life, walking in the light of God's word.

Reasons for rejection (2:6-11)

About 740 BC, Announcement of judgment. We must be very careful in studying this section of God's Word. Several parts of the Hebrew text are difficult to read. Verse 6b reads literally: "They are full from the east and diviners as the Philistines." Translators usually add a word very similar to "from the east" meaning diviners. The word translated "strike hands with" occurs only here, so its meaning is not really known. The Dead Sea Scrolls do not contain verses 9b-10.

Isaiah spoke to a people who were rich and told them why they were to be ruined. They listened to magicians rather than prophets, practiced foreign rites, worshiped foreign gods, then strutted proudly around wondering why God was displeased. Traditionally, the prophet's task had been to plead to God on behalf of the people. The situation had become so desperate Isaiah could only raise the terrifying curse: "forgive them not!" (v. 9). Then he called to the people to hide from God's terror. The ironical advice underlines the fact of no escape.

The oracle points back ("in that day," v. 11) to the opening of the chapter to remind the readers that no one is guaranteed a part in the "latter days" (v. 2). God is the only one sure to be exalted then.

Preaching Against Pride (2:12-22)

About 740 BC, Prophecy of disaster. Isaiah joined Amos in transforming a favorite expression of the popular piety. Everyone believed the day of Yahweh, Israel's God, would be a day of victory in battle against her enemies. The prophets said it would be a day of victory for Yahweh against his enemies, his own people (Amos 5:18-20). Isaiah underlined his previous condemnation of the people of God. God's day is victory only for those who are truly God's people, not for the proud.

Verses 20-21 extend the description. The idols people made to worship were fit only for the animals who inhabited the darkest places of the earth. The prophet concluded with another curse,

calling his faithful followers to give up on human beings because
they were only dust given the breath of life by God (see the same
expression in Gen. 2:7). A sarcastic rhetorical question is a fitting
conclusion. People have no basis for pride. In the end they will
crawl trembling into the cave to finish their days.

A Lack of Leadership (3:1-12)

740 BC, Prophecy of disaster climaxing in woe oracles. Again
the Hebrew text calls us to be cautious. "Magician" (v. 3) is
translated "skilled craftsman" by earliest translators (see NIV), but
today it is usually understood in light of Aramaic and Syrian words
meaning *magician.* The word translated "Babes" (v. 4) occurs only
here and Isaiah 66:4, where it means "ill-treatment, affliction,
capricious use of power." Thus NEB: "who shall govern as the fancy
takes them." "Healer" (v. 7) represents a play on a word that means
"to tie up" and can be used both to tie up a wound and to saddle (be
in the saddle), thus to rule (compare NEB, "I will not be your
master"). "Partiality" (v. 9) occurs only here in the Bible, so its
meaning is uncertain. A quick glance at several translations will
reveal the difficulty of translating verse 12. The first half may mean
"Taskmasters oppress them" or "a child oppresses them" (AT). There
follows either "Money-lenders rule over them" or "women rule over
them" (AT).

The central message of the text is clear. Not only religion, but also
rulers formed Israel's pride problem. For leaders who simply
seduced and swallowed God's people (v. 12), God had a remedy:
Assyrian exile. Isaiah described this exile in some detail. The
leaders of every area of the country's life—religious, political, legal,
military—were snatched from their culture and home and sprinkled
over the far reaches of the Assyrian empire. This left the land totally
at the mercy of foreign governors. Experienced local leadership was
nonexistent.

Amid Judah's pride in her prosperity, the prophet described her
imminent fate. Siege warfare would remove all food supplies. Then
exile would remove the leadership. Inexperienced leadership would
lead to anarchy. Ranks and values in society would flip-flop upside-
down (v. 5). The only qualification for the highest position in the land
would be possession of life's necessities, but the nominee would lie
and connive to avoid election (vv. 6-7). All this would happen
because God's people had acted like little children, defiantly

disobeying God, even when his glory stood revealed before their eyes (v. 8). So brazen and proud were they, that they flaunted their sin openly. Sodom offered the only possible comparison.

In face of such pride and flagrant rebellion, the divine response is especially noteworthy. God entered into mourning for his people, taking up the funeral lamentation for them (9b). He offered instructions of hope for the righteous remnant (v. 10), then resumed his mourning tones to announce the judgment of the wicked (v. 11). Lack of leadership was both the cause and result of their situation. This brought divine judgment and a real sense of loss in the heart of God.

Princes Prey on the Paupers (3:13-15)

740 BC, Courtroom trial. In his speech patterns, the prophet moved from the funeral home to the courtroom as he condemned the leaders of the people. Cleverly, the prophet pictured the divine judge standing in the courtroom ready to judge "peoples" (see v. 13, RSV margin). His audience stood immediately to attention, eager to hear the prophet proclaim the expected word of judgment on the enemies. (The RSV translation follows the early Greek and Syriac in changing the Hebrew text from "peoples" to "his people," thus missing the rhetorical skill of the prophet.) Only with verse 14 would the audience suddenly awake to what was happening. The prophet placed his audience under arrest and dragged them into God's courtroom for judgment and sentencing.

Primary focus is on the leadership. The elders originally formed the governing body of the nomadic tribe. Settled in the land, they assumed the function of elders in the Canaanite cities (Josh. 9:11) making political decisions. As such, they functioned in making tribal decisions. In national affairs they became advisors to the king. In Ruth 4, elders functioned as the local court of justice in the city gate. Laws for this function appear in Deuteronomy 19:11-12; 21:1-9,18-21; 22:13-21; 25:5-10. But in Isaiah's day the elders used their legal and political powers to feather their own nests, becoming a major factor in God's judgment upon Israel.

The "princes" contributed their part to the problem. They were royal officials, who traced their positions of power back to Moses (Ex. 18:25, where "heads" is the Hebrew term for "princes"). As such they had rigid qualifications (Ex. 18:21). They were military officials. They had power to imprison people (1 Kings 22:26).

Gradually the term came to be generalized to include all royal officials (1 Kings 4:2). At times they represented a threat to the king (Jer. 38:24-27). They also represented a threat to the poor country farmers, using their political power to demand payments and gifts. Farmers who did not pay found their vineyards burned. Isaiah bluntly called this stealing.

The elders and princes saw no significance in such oppressive acts (v. 15). God saw ultimate meaning, forming the basis for his condemnation of the nation to destruction. "Says the Lord" (v. 15) represents a technical expression for "oracle of Yahweh" which occurs 365 times in the Bible, most often in the prophetic literature to lend authority to the prophetic word, since that word was not usually believed by the audience. On Lord of hosts, see 1:21-26.

Too Late for the Ladies (3:16 to 4:1)

740 BC, Prophecy of disaster. The courage of the prophet knew no limits. He even attacked the Jerusalem women's circle. In so doing, he used a vocabulary that is not met in other biblical books, so the translation remains quite uncertain at many points. The student of the Bible should compare several translations. Again, the punishment pronounced on the proud prancers of Zion matched the crime. Lovely hairdos would fall down as scratching fingers struck angrily at dandruff or a more serious scalp disorder. "Lay bare their secret parts" (v. 17) probably should be translated "expose their head," that is, make them bald. Then God would remove all the feminine finery (vv. 18-23), not necessarily because it was evil in itself, but because it was contributing to the false pride. New clothing would be laid out, that suitable for a pilgrimage into exile rather than a pilgrimage to the Temple as was described in verse 16. Such a pilgrimage would be lonely, for the men would die in battle (v. 25). Funeral rites would be the only social activity (v. 26).

The women would lose all their pride in an all-out fight over whatever sort of man happened to remain alive. The women would want no material goods from the man, only a married name and children to remove the disgrace of being unmarried and barren.

Protection for the Pious (4:2-6)

Prediction of hope. "That day" cannot be totally dark (compare 3:10). This section of the book thus ends, as it began, with a note of hope (see 2:1-5). The date of "that day" remains vague and undefined. The point is not to circle a day on a calendar but to affirm the saving purpose of God for his people. The only chronological note is that such salvation comes after judgment.

A bouquet of images describes the day of hope. First, agricultural language describes the blossoming and fertility of the trees for the remnant left in the land. Such language had wider overtones. The "branch" or "sprout" is related to the verb "sprout" connected with kingship hopes in 2 Samuel 23:5 and Psalm 132:17. The noun designated the hoped-for king who would bring salvation (Jer. 23:5; 33:15; Zech. 3:8; 6:12). Thus Judaism early used this passage as a basis of future hopes for a king. Survivors (v. 2) form the root of salvation hope in 10:20 and 37:31-32. It is a military term (Gen. 32:9; 2 Sam. 15:14). "He who is left" (v. 3) appears in different forms twenty-seven times in Isaiah with the double meaning of disaster and hope. Here it points to the hope that a chance for survival and new life remained.

This remnant hope ranges through much of the Old Testament literature (see Gen. 7:23; 45:7; 1 Kings 19:9-18; Amos 5:15). Here such a remnant will be declared "holy." This reflects cultic practice by which the priest declared a worshiper fit to enter the Temple and worship (see Lev. 17—26, particularly ch. 19; Ex. 22:31). Isaiah said no priest would proclaim man holy. Nor could ethical actions provide such holiness. God himself must perform the cleansing, which can be done only through acts of judgment and destruction (v. 4). Those chosen for inclusion among the remnant are "recorded for life in Jerusalem" (3b). This is a figure of speech taken from the political practice of taking a census and recording family trees (see Neh. 7:64).

The prophet turned to creation language in verse 5. Hope for the remnant lay only in the power of God to start all over again and give his preserved people a new place to live. The glory of the place is the protective presence of God symbolized as in the Exodus event. Not just the holy of holies in the Temple (1 Kings 8:10-11), but the entire site of Mount Zion would become God's dwelling place on earth. The concluding statements (5b-6) represent a very difficult text, reading literally: "for upon all glory a shelter, a booth will be for a shade daily from devastating heat and for a refuge from cloudburst and from rain" (AT). The glory of the divine presence is thus roofed in so that it remains with Jerusalem and cannot depart (compare Ezek. 10:18-19). Israel would find protection from all life's threats.

Such protection is not dependent upon human leaders or pride. Divine presence guarantees it, removing all reason for human pride.

Redeeming the Remnant (5:1 to 11:16)

Two major types of prophetic literature appear in the next section of the book. Poetic oracles (5:1-30 and 9:1 to 11:16) surround prose stories about the prophet (6:1 to 8:22). These have been artistically joined together. The woe statements of 5:8-23 are resumed in 10:1-4, and the chorus of 5:25 reappears in 9:12,17,21; 10:4. Prophetic condemnation and judgment again provide the bulk of the material, but the climax shows that hope and salvation for a remnant is the controlling theme (10:5 to 11:16).

Vindication Against the Vineyard (5:1-7)

740 BC, Harvest love song changed ironically into a courtroom trial. We stand before one of the great pieces of prophetic literature, indeed, one of the greatest pieces of literature ever written. The prophet donned the actor's grease paint to perform for his audience. He sang a love song, fitting into the frivolous mood of gaiety permeating the harvest holidays. In so doing, he assumed the role of the friend of the bridegroom, who represented the groom before the bride, since the bride and groom were not allowed to see one another before the wedding. He used the language of agriculture, a common custom in Israelite love poetry (see the Song of Sol.). He showed the faithfulness of the bridegroom in preparing every detail. Thus the bridegroom had great expectations (v. 2*b*). Suddenly the prophet changed his mood and image. He called the court into session (v. 3) with the citizens of his country as the jury. First, he put the bridegroom in the defendant's chair (v. 4). Then he quickly pronounced the verdict (v. 5). The bride was guilty! The sentence: death! (vv. 5-6). Abruptly, the prophet changed his speech form once more. He interpreted the entire love song-court trial as a parable, indeed an allegory. Yahweh, the God of Israel, was the bridegroom; Judah, the bride. God's expectation is described in beautiful alliteration, which might be rendered: "He waited for righteousness, but here are riots; for legality, but here is lamentation" (AT). The divine lover had suffered ultimate disappointment and rejection, and he must discipline his beloved (compare Hos. 1—3).

Woes on the Worldly (5:8-30)

740 BC, Woe oracles. The note of condemnation and death does not come easily to the prophet nor to God. As so often, the funeral mourning cry of "Woe, alas, how horrible!" follows. We have here a series of such woe oracles just as in Isaiah 28—31, Habakkuk 2, and Amos 5—6. A few points in the text provide difficulties. Verse 9 reads literally, "By (or in) my ears, Yahweh of Hosts," (AT) which must be an abbreviated oath formula. Translators must supply some verb of swearing. "Dying of hunger" (v. 13) is the reading of the earliest translations; the Hebrew text reading is "its honored ones are men of hunger" (AT). The Hebrew probably seeks to make a word play between two words "men" and "dying," which share similar appearance and sound. Verse 17 is filled with rare words and forms, giving rise to many possible translations. I think the proper translation is, "The lambs will graze as if it were their pasture, while strangers eat the ruins of the fatlings," (AT) but note the variety among modern translations and commentaries.

The grammar and syntax of verses 25-30 present great uncertainty. Some translations place the events in the future tense, others in the present, and still others in the past. The Hebrew word ending verse 30 occurs only here in the Bible and is of uncertain meaning: suggestions include clouds, hilltops, and shadows.

Uncertainties aside, the passage pours judgment upon a prosperous people so intent on gaining wealth and enjoying themselves they ignore the real world. They have robbed the poor farmers through unjust economic practices and have taken farms until they have only a lovely country mansion with no neighbors (v. 8). They have eaten and drunk so much at the Temple parties that they do not miss the guest of honor, when God departs to bring judgment upon them (v. 12).

God's judgment is appropriate to the crime. Mansions become lonely haunted houses (v. 9). The work of the farmer produces only one-tenth the expected crop (v. 10). Landed nobility march into exile, their feasting turned to enforced fasting (v. 13). Only Sheol, the home of the dead, finds its appetite satisfied (v. 14).

The contrast is complete. The mighty of Judah have been "humbled" (v. 15), while the very action of God in judgment has proved the pure holiness and righteousness of God. God stands "exalted" (v. 16). The Promised Land and Holy City are reduced to occupation by flocks and foreigners (v. 17).

The situation became even worse. The people were so occupied in their evil that they taunted the prophet and his God, daring God to act, thus implying that God no longer had power to act (vv. 18-19). The prophet claimed that they had their priorities upside down (v. 20). In Genesis Adam and Eve sought the power to decide good and evil for themselves (3:5-6). Isaiah said his generation had totally confused the two things. This could be seen in their uncontrolled use of liquor and their mockery of the system of social justice (vv. 22-23). The ominous prophetic "therefore" sounds forth twice (vv. 24-25) to predict punishment on God's worldly-wise, but wicked, people. The divine wrath would become insatiable (v. 25b). God would whistle for Assyria to come (v. 26). The sounds and fury of warfare would thunder over the land. Hope had vanished for that generation.

Called to Condemn (6:1-13)

740 BC, Prophetic call narrative. A brief moment of biography provides a glimpse of how such dire predictions came to be uttered. The basic explanation comes from God's commission to his prophetic messenger. This occurred within the Jerusalem Temple (v. 1), perhaps indicating that the prophet had been a professional minister on the Temple staff. The earthly Temple was suddenly transformed for the prophet to enter the heavenly court, where God's ministers were serving him (v. 2). Seraphim are literally the searing or burning ones and appear only here in the Old Testament as members of God's court.

The heavenly council is one of many ideas Israel had in common with its Near Eastern neighbors. Other religions saw a king of the gods ruling over a council of lesser gods. Israel claimed that her God, Yahweh, the only real God, ruled over a group of beings who served him, particularly in the role of messengers. (See Job 1:6; 1 Kings 22:19.) Israel also made the radical assertion that God was the king of the nation rather than simply king of the gods.

The setting of Isaiah's call was the doxology sung responsively by two members of the heavenly court. They looked down upon the earth and saw that it reflected the divine glory—that is, the prestige, wealth, and honor of God, literally, his weightiness. (For divine holiness, see the comments on 1:4.) The prophet quickly realized that he had no business in such a holy setting. He was able to see what was forbidden even to Moses (Ex. 33:20). Isaiah was not, however, the first to see God (Gen. 16:13; 32:31; Judg. 6:22; 13:22; Pss. 11:7; 17:15; 27:4; 42:2; 63:2).

The vision turned Isaiah's eyes inward to realize his own sinfulness. He used the "woe" language of the funeral to pronounce his own mourning at what appeared to be his own certain death. "I am lost" (v. 5) may mean "I am silenced, still, cannot reply," (AT) since this is most often the meaning of the Hebrew word.

The prophet stood in the divine council but identified himself with his people on earth. He and his people were unclean, a term used in the Temple worship. The heavenly ministers of Yahweh performed the proper rituals for Isaiah (v. 7). Here the dynamic character of Old Testament worship dramatizes both the disastrous nature of sin before God and the power of God to forgive and forget.

Isaiah was fully accepted into the heavenly council before God. He heard the question posed by God to the holy council, "Who will go for us?" Rather than let one of the seraphim answer (1 Kings 22:21), Isaiah himself boldly volunteered, only to receive an impossible assignment—the hardening of Israel. Here is the Old Testament's bluntest statement of God's total freedom over his world. As God once hardened Pharaoh (Ex. 7—14), so he hardened his enemy Israel. Here human understanding must bow before the sovereignty of God and his purposes with people. Jesus took up the same words and applied them to his generation (Matt. 13:10-15). At times, God must destroy a generation before he can work out his purpose of salvation. In so doing, he gives his messenger a hard word of judgment which leads neither to a great following among the people nor personal happiness.

The prophet backed away from the task, asking "How long?" The divine answer painted an ugly picture: total destruction (vv. 11-12)! Verse 13 apparently gives a glimmer of hope in the darkness, but the text is almost impossible to read (compare the translations of RSV, NEB, KJV). Most of the language belongs to the high places of worship with holy trees and stones, yet it appears to picture repeated destruction leading to a "holy seed."

Chapter 6 serves as a foundation stone to prove the authority of the prophetic preaching. Isaiah did not preach destruction from his own insidious desires but from the deep conviction of a call experience with God. The prophet shrank from the task and pleaded for his people, but God sent him out to accomplish divine, not human, purposes.

Confrontations Amid Crisis (7:1 to 9:7)

The biographical report continues, turning to experiences of the prophet amid royalty and nobility. These show that the prophet faithfully carried out his commission. His message achieved exactly what God said (ch. 6), hardening the heart of the people and their king.

Faith or failure (7:1-9).—*733 BC, Prophetic report.* Facing Assyrian pressure, Rezin, the king of Syria, gained support from the usurper Pekah of Israel (2 Kings 15:25), then beckoned to Judah to join. Ahaz, the young king, refused. Rezin and Pekah besieged Jerusalem to force Ahaz to join forces against Assyria. In the midst of decision, Ahaz met the prophet Isaiah, who came at God's command (v. 3). Isaiah took with him his son who bore the ominous, symbolic name "A remnant shall return." This is a play on words. "Remnant" may mean a hopeless handful or the basis for a new society. "Return" may point to literal returning from war or to spiritual return, being the normal Hebrew word for repent. In the military setting, the name suggested defeat in battle. The child's presence was a warning to the king not to enter battle, as well as a challenge to God's people to be part of the repentant remnant.

The geographical setting of the confrontation (v. 3) was apparently outside the city at a good place to examine the military situation. God's word for the situation is clear, an oracle of salvation (v. 4) calling on the king to do nothing. His enemies had burned themselves out and were simply dying embers.

Verse 5 has an opening formula "Because" which introduces a new oracle. It describes the situation for the following sermon. The situation was desperate for Ahaz. The enemies sought to replace him with a "son of Tabeel," that is, a man with an Aramaic name and, thus, Aramaic connections. He would be more open to the plans of his Syrian countrymen.

The prophetic messenger formula, "Thus says the Lord," (v. 7) introduced the divine decision and affirmed that the weak opposition kings would not succeed, since they depended on their political position and not on God. The prophet turned to the king and his advisers with God's plan, which is expressed in a word play on the

Hebrew word meaning both to believe, and also to be established, made stable. We can translate: "If you all do not confirm (this), you will not be confirmed" (AT). Royal reaction is not reported.

The poetic oracle is interrupted by a prosaic interpretation in verse 8b, pointing to a time sixty-five years hence when Ephraim, the Northern Kingdom, would see its national identity dashed to pieces. This apparently pointed to 671 BC when foreigners settled the northern country (Ezra 4:2,10), though Israel had lost all political power by 722 BC. It added a specific threat against the Northern Kingdom to the warning to the southern king.

Confounding conception (7:10-17).—Prophetic report. The king had not heard God's final word. Isaiah confronted Ahaz again. The king could display his faith by asking God for a sign which would confirm the divine help. Here is a unique example of a prophet given opportunity to prove his word true immediately. The Hebrew text of verse 11b is not clear, reading, "Go deep, ask, or go high to the heights" (AT). Most translators change the text slightly, such as the RSV reading (compare NEB, NIV).

Alas, the king refused the offer, but with the most pious language. "Who am I to test God?" (AT). God did not want pious language. He sought faith. Ahaz was too busy working his poor people until they were dead tired. The prophet charged that his pious language made God just as tired. God would act on his own and give the king a sign.

The sign is given in the traditional manner of announcing the birth of a child (Gen. 16:11; Judg. 13:3,5). The birth would be a sign for the king in the immediate circumstances. The Hebrew text reads, "The young woman has conceived and is giving birth to a son" (v. 14, AT). (See NEB, TEV, RSV note.) The Septuagint interpreted this, "The virgin will conceive," a translation taken up in Matthew 1:23 and the continuing Christian tradition.

Ahaz probably knew the woman of whom the prophet spoke. It may even have been one of his own wives, since this would have been the surprise fulfillment of the oracle, a royal prince becoming a sign to the king, his name constantly reminding the king that "God is with us." Such a sign would give hope to a king who trusted God, but would be a constant threat to one who followed his own strategy.

Verse 15 continues the ambiguous word play, for the food is that of extreme blessing and paradise in some ancient contexts, but that of poor nomads in others. In the present context, it would appear to be a promise of blessing for the child in the near future. Promise for the child would mean judgment on the enemy kings (v. 16). With these words of hope, Ahaz prepared to bid the prophet adieu, but Isaiah had one last word. The prophet well knew the obstinate mind-set of the king. The result was obvious. Judgment would come to Judah, too. The prophet used shocking words to announce it. Isaiah compared this judgment to the rebellion of the Northern Kingdom separating from Judah in 928 BC (1 Kings 12). The instrument of judgment was also clear, the king of Assyria, who threatened not only Syria and Israel, but also Judah.

Poor Ahaz would not listen. The cringing king was afraid to trust his fathers' faithful God and ran rebelliously to the royalty of Assyria for help (2 Kings 16:7-9). But the prophet did not simply bury his word along with his hopes for Ahaz. Rather, he preserved it among his followers (8:16), waiting for a new royal child, who would come from a family of faith and show that God's intention was to bestow his gracious blessing on humanity. The people of God waited seven hundred years before such a child was born. Even then, the paradise remained a promise. The church continues waiting for that day.

Day of destruction (7:18-25).—To make sure the meaning of the previous section was totally clear, a series of oracles follows explicitly defining the expected day of disaster. Traditional enemies would come from north and south (Hos. 9:3; 11:5; Jer. 2:36). Assyria would give Judah a shave too close for comfort (v. 20). A herdsman would have only three animals left after the devastation (v. 21), but God would be with the poor and supply food from the milk of these animals and with honey (v. 22). The rich farmer, however, would see his vineyards become weed patches, even though their price made them the most valuable in the land. The only people using the land would be hunters seeking wild game (v. 24). Otherwise, the land would be left to animals searching desperately for a morsel to eat among the thorns and briers. What a day God has for a king and his people who will not believe!

Child of condemnation (8:1-4).—*713 BC, Prophetic report of symbolic act.* The prophet interpreted the birth of his own son as a sign from God. Before the birth, God called upon the prophet to prepare a public billboard, "Belonging to Speedy is the spoil, quick the plunder" (AT). But who is speeding, and who forms the "spoil"? The sign is ambivalent. Will Judah plunder her enemies, or the enemies Judah? Certainly, the prophet hoped the sign would mean salvation for Judah, but he knew the demand placed on the king for faith. We can be sure the king also knew! The prophet worked his way through all the legal red tape, getting two witnesses (Deut. 17:6; 19:15). And what witnesses—the leading priest of the Temple (2 Kings 16:10-11) and a Zechariah, who may even have been the king's father-in-law (2 Kings 18:2). Isaiah had access to high circles, another sign that he may have been employed in the Temple (see ch. 6 notes). He was also married to a woman who may have worked on the Temple staff as a prophetess. The birth event gave clearer indication of the meaning of the sign. Before the child began to say his first "Mommy, Daddy," the king of Assyria would do away with all claims to power made by Judah's two enemies.

River of rage (8:5-8).—733 BC, Prediction of disaster. That the sign was not totally good for Judah becomes clear in the next word from the prophet, given only a little while later. The Hebrew of verse 6*b*, uses a word that normally means joy, rejoicing (see Isa. 24:8,11; 32:13; 60:15; 62:5; Jer. 49:25). Here and in Job 8:19 the word may be related to one which sounds much the same and means "to lose courage." Compare various translations.

The picture is one of siege in which God provided a good water supply and protection within the city of Jerusalem. The people refused to trust God's protection, preferring Assyria. So the prophet described Assyria—a mighty flood, branching out until it covered Judah. The only reaction is the cry, "Oh, Immanuel" (v. 8), referring to the sign of 7:14 and interpreting it as a negative sign. God is with us in destructive rage. Yet at the same time, the cry remained a prayer, hoping for divine intervention. Again we see the power of the prophet to use language with double meanings.

Present to protect (8:9-10).—733 BC, Sarcastic use of a military call to battle. Using military language, the prophet summoned the nations to fight and lose. Again, this gave hope to his own people. The basis of such hope is Immanuel, "God is with us." But it is a hope after defeat and destruction. God would be present to judge his people, then to judge the nations.

Falling before our fear (8:11-15).—733 BC, Prophetic teaching. The prophet imitated the priest, whose duty it was to teach the people how to behave before the holy God. He subtly turned the teaching into a word of judgment. "Warned me" should probably be read with the Dead Sea Scrolls' "restrained me, turned me from." The prophet set himself apart from his people. God had given him a new life-style. This was the basis for his new teaching. The new life-style centered in a new politics, for crisis had produced panic. Everyone was on the outlook for traitors. The least word or action beyond the normal aroused the cry, "Conspiracy . . . conspiracy." Within Judah, an Assyrian party faced a Syrian party, which in turn faced a Yahweh party. The level of trust was very low.

The voice of Yahweh called for calm and trust, not panic and fear. No enemy king is worth the time spent worrying, plotting, or trembling in fear. In fact, only the holy God deserves our fear. Here is the most obvious of the many word plays in this section. Fear of God is, of course, a central concept in the divine-human relationship, but the particular Hebrew term used here appears elsewhere only in Malachi 1:6; 2:5 to designate this relationship. Normally, it expresses the horrible terrors of war. This war terminology is used deliberately by Isaiah to make a word play within the military context. The same type of word play occurs in Psalm 71:11. Judah must not fear the terrors of war, but her "Holy Terror."

The military context also determines the use of the Lord of hosts title with its reference to God as the commander of the armies. A similar word play occurs here in the use of "sanctuary" (v. 14). This is literally a holy place where the holy God is worshiped. It can also mean the place where a person fleeing from his enemies seeks sanctuary. God is often called Israel's Rock. Israel and Judah would stumble on the rock. Without faith, Israel would fall.

Tie up the teaching (8:16-22).—*733 BC, Prophetic instruction.* Knowing he would win the war, Isaiah realized when he had lost a battle. He retreated from confrontation with king and people into the sanctuary of his faithful followers. He devoted his time to teaching his students. He had faith in the words he had uttered and wanted them preserved for a day when they would be heeded. God provided faithful disciples who took the first step in canonizing Isaiah's prophecy.

Even when he did not preach, Isaiah remained faithful to his prophetic commission. His very presence with his sons, who bore symbolic names (7:3; 8:3), recalled every word of his message to the king and his counselors. In silence, Isaiah exercised his prophetic office.

People should have sought the will of God from Isaiah, but Judah ran to mediums who thought they could consult the dead and find the fate of the living (compare 1 Sam. 28). Isaiah said the peeps of birds were all they found. Yet, such mediums reigned supreme in the crisis situation. They put the true prophet out of work. But not for long! Isaiah knew God would act to bring fulfillment to the prophetic word, and people would come running to him again.

This faith was expressed in verse 20, whose exact meaning remains hidden, as a glance at several translations will show. In some way, it reflects the superiority of Isaiah's preaching to the words of the wizards. In such a situation, the prophet could only draw a picture of the famine and hunger sure to follow the inevitable defeat (vv. 21-22). Here again the Hebrew text is difficult. We do not know who the subject is nor where the action takes place. Gloom, darkness, and anger dominate. The prohibition of cursing in Exodus 22:28 is broken. Despair has brought the subject to doubt both the king and God as leaders of the people. "In the former time" is an introductory formula, and 9:1a repeats the vocabulary of the preceding section; so 9:1a probably concludes 8:16-22.

Sons of salvation (9:1-7).—732 BC, Thanksgiving. Verse 1 is prose, while verses 2-7 are poetry. The first verse serves to join the previous picture of darkness with the light that follows. To do so, it contrasts the former situation with the new hope. The Assyrians had annexed both the northeastern (Naphtali—Josh. 19:32-39) and the northwestern (Zebulun—Josh. 19:10-16) portions of the Northern Kingdom in 732 BC. The prophet, stepping out of his Jerusalem context for a moment, spoke a word of hope to the north. A new day was coming. Turning to use the Assyrian geographical divisions—"way of the sea, land beyond the Jordan, Galilee of the nations" (v. 1)—the prophet depicted a new glory. The basis of this glory is now explained in verses 2-7.

Verse 2 introduces a song of thanksgiving. Harvest and military language join to praise the new act of God. Verse 5 shows us that the great reason for rejoicing is not military victory. Such lies still in the future and is guaranteed by the event which has actually happened. What has happened is the birth of a son. Here is a royal birth announcement. For once the prophet and king stood together, rejoicing over the happy event. A touch of irony appeared in the prophet's voice as he looked at the baby and saw in him, not in his father, the hope of the nation. Yes, even in joining the royal family's thanksgiving, the prophet succeeded in condemning Ahaz. The only good thing about the present king was that he would eventually pass away to make way for Judah's new hope.

The Psalms show us that the names used for the new baby belong to the Judean understanding of kingship. The king devised plans and counsel which were too wonderful for men, almost like God (compare 2 Sam. 16:23), for ultimately it is God who is wonderful in counsel. "Mighty God" (v. 6) or "Heroic God" reflects the same type of thinking as Psalm 45:6, where the Hebrew text addresses the king as "god." This reflects the respect and authority due the king as distinguished from other men and his closeness to Yahweh, the only God. Psalm 2:7 shows that the king was adopted as "son" of God when he ascended the throne (see Ps. 89:26-27; 2 Sam. 7:14). Thus a title "Mighty God," which belongs only to God in its real meaning can be transferred to the obedient king. "Everlasting Father" is unexpected as a title for a newborn child. This is one reason many interpreters have referred the poem to the coronation ceremony rather than the birth of the king. But the prophet here announced birth, not adoption, and gave the traditional royal titles in expectation of the coming child and as judgment over against what the reigning king had not fulfilled.

The new king would truly be the Father of his country rather than the servant of Assyria. For him the people could truly wish an everlasting reign and life, as they traditionally did for kings. "Prince of Peace" reflects the role of the king in all areas of the nation's life. Peace is the opposite of war. It is a sense of personal well-being. It is also material prosperity.

The prophet joined the king in rejoicing at the new birth, for now the country truly had hopes that the promises to David would be fulfilled. The new king would be "Great in Dominion" (AT) bringing lasting peace to the throne of David. But such lasting peace was dependent upon a king whose chief ends are "with justice and with righteousness" (v. 7). Justice is the center of the prophetic demand on the people of God. But the same Hebrew word also means the law which establishes justice (Isa. 26:9), the correct teaching (28:26), and the judgment which enforces the law (4:4). Justice ultimately does not rest on human law or judgment, but upon the nature of God (5:16).

The prophetic hope here thus rests not on the power of the new king, but upon the "zeal of the Lord of hosts" (v. 7). This zeal is at the same time jealousy. It is a term which in the ancient Near East referred to the relationship between the gods, one god being jealous of another. Israel used it to describe God's attitude toward his own worshipers, a usage not known elsewhere in Israel's environment.

This attitude is the foundation of the Ten Commandments prohibiting worship of any other gods (Ex. 20:5). Such jealousy brings judgment upon a disobedient people. But suffering under judgment, Israel could pray in hope on the basis of divine jealousy (Isa. 63:15) and find God acting in zeal and jealousy to restore his people (Isa. 37:32). In our passage, the jealousy and zealousness of God is the hope for Israel's kingship. Only when God chooses to act will the people of God find the hoped-for king reigning over them.

Isaiah hoped the newborn baby would be the final realization of the long-awaited fulfillment of the promises to David. But this new baby did not fill the prophetic demands. Thus when the prophet tucked his teaching away among his disciples (8:16), this prophecy, too, was tucked away to await a new baby. The people of God had to wait over seven hundred years for Jesus of Nazareth who did fulfill and even surpass such expectations. He did not bring all to immediate fulfillment, but set his followers on a course of expectation looking to the final coming of the Prince of Peace.

The Abiding Anger of the Almighty (9:8 to 10:4)

734 BC, A prophecy of disaster against the Northern Kingdom. This passage is quite distinctive in Isaiah because its subject is the Northern Kingdom rather than the Southern. We must understand the situation of the prophet, however, as being a minister to the south. This means that Isaiah 9:8 to 10:4 is really an oracle against a foreign nation, similar to those found in chapters 13—23. Such sermons were addressed rhetorically to the enemy. Yet the enemy never heard them. The audience that listened was the prophet's own people. When he pronounced judgment on the enemy, he was normally proclaiming salvation for his people. We have seen in 7:4-9,16 and 8:4 that Isaiah promised salvation to Judah in the midst of the war with Syria and Ephraim. Such salvation, however, was connected with the demand for faith and ultimately accompanied by judgment upon Judah because she would not believe, relying instead upon Assyria. The chorus (9:12,17,21; 10:4) joins the section to 5:24-25, while the woe oracle in 10:1-4 connects back to the series in 5:8-23. This consciously ties the present section back to chapter 5. Why? The writer wanted to show that the judgments applied also to the south. By itself, 9:8 to 10:4 could be read as hope for the south and judgment only for the north. Pointing it back to chapter 5 shows that judgment was pronounced on the south also, because Judah imitated the action of the north and had to repeat its history.

The change of tenses in verse 8 shows that God had spoken, but the judgment had not yet "fallen" (v. 10). Word of God was sent as a messenger which brought to pass that which it proclaimed. Jacob, Israel, Ephraim, and Samaria are distinctive ways of referring to the Northern Kingdom by reference to its patriarch (Gen. 35:10), its official national name, its major tribe, and its capital city. The prophet left no doubt about his attitude to the north: they were proud and arrogant. Only God has a right to such majesty and pride. The pride is seen in their contempt for God's discipline. He had defeated and destroyed. They thought they could build everything back with better materials.

Verses 11-12 read in the Hebrew: "Yahweh has lifted up the enemies of Rezin; against him and his foes he provokes (or will provoke). Syria from the east and Philistines on the west! They have eaten Israel with a whole mouth" (AT). The two statements are unclear. Most translations and commentaries change the text, omitting Rezin (RSV, NEB, TEV, but see NIV, KJV). The problem was seen early. The early Greek translators turned the verses to read "God will dash down those who rise up against him on Mount Zion and shall scatter his enemies—Syria and the Philistines, who eat up Israel." It appears that verse 11 was originally an oracle against Syria and its king Rezin. Verse 12 then turns this against Israel.

God's punishment of his people had a definite purpose. He sought repentance, which would turn his people back to him away from other gods (v. 13). To repent carries with it the spiritual meaning, but also the meaning of traveling back to one's country. One is the result of the other. Repentance has a still greater effect, for it restores relationship with God. In this section the chorus echoes the sad complaint that God had not returned, because the people had not. Instead, God extended his judgment, eliminating the leadership of the people (vv. 14-16). The result was that God had turned from his normal course of action. He no longer rejoiced over the strong young warriors, nor did he express compassion and concern for the widows and orphans, who could normally depend upon his special protection.

Israel did not turn to God, and so God would not turn to them. Instead, his judgment burned the land (v. 18). Still, Israel paid no heed. She fought among herself for political leadership (v. 21), or she turned against her brothers in the kingdom of Judah. God did discipline, but to no avail. All that remained for the prophet was to whine out his funeral song in mourning over his dying people (10:1-4). Their evil conduct left no doubt about their future—exile! (v. 4). The implication of the last part of verse 4 is that the remainder of God's people, Judah, are next in line!

Anger with Assyria (10:5 to 11:16)

Rattling the rod (10:5-19).—705 BC, *Ironical woe oracle*. The woe does continue. "Woe" in verse 1 and "Ah" in verse 5 translate the same Hebrew term. Unexpectedly, the subject is Assyria, not Judah. Verse 5b reads literally: "A staff! It is in their hand my fury" (AT). This explains the role of Assyria in punishing God's people.

Assyria was God's secret agent. She did not know herself that Yahweh was using her. She proudly attributed her success to her own power and purpose. For her, all nations she captured were the same. Assyria captured the Syrian cities of Calno (738 BC), Carchemish (717 BC), Hamath (738 BC and again 720 BC), and Arpad (740 BC and 720 BC). Damascus was, of course, the capital city of Rezin, while Samaria was the capital of Israel. All were alike to Assyria. Isaiah knew better. Yahweh alone gave Assyria permission to attack Samaria.

Suddenly, the prophet stabbed his Judean audience in the back (v. 12). The great Syrian cities with their famous gods fell. Samaria was no different. She, too, had relied on similar gods, but ones with less reputation and history than those of Syria. And, the prophet shouts, Jerusalem is also no different! She, too, will fall! Only then would God punish Assyria. The prophetic irony is complete. The mourning cry over the enemy, raising hopes in the hearts of his Judean listeners, turned into a blazing threat against Judah for its idolatry.

Still, the climax was a threat against proud Assyria (vv. 13-19). Assyria was compared to a forest burned so completely that a child could scribble the number of trees left.

It should be noted that "like a bull I have brought down those who sat on thrones" (v. 13) is only one of the many possible translations. Check various translations.

Rewarding the remnant (10:20-27).—Here remnant theology is interpreted precisely. Remnant theology has two sides. God disciplined the nation which leaned on Assyria for help until she had to turn back to God. Such return had to be in truth, in loyal faithfulness. Such a remnant fulfilled the name of the prophet's son (7:3) but reflected only a shadow of former glory (v. 22), since God's righteous judgment had to be completed (v. 23). Once such judgment was finished, an oracle of salvation could be sounded (v. 24) showing that the God of the Exodus from Egypt and of the judges could repeat his former victories for Israel. Then Assyria would no longer be a burden oppressing Israel. Remnant theology thus presupposes almost total destruction before God acts to create a new community out of the faithful few.

Marching to murder (10:28-32).—*712 BC, Battle report with prophetic warning.* The Assyrian army of King Sargon repelled rebellions in Philistia, centering in Ashdod from 713-11 BC (compare ch. 20). Apparently, Sargon sent troops from the north to make sure Jerusalem did not become involved. The prophet imitated a military scout's report as he warned Jerusalem of the approach.

Pruning the powerful (10:33-34).—Isaiah then issued a warning, which he left intentionally open to interpretation. He pictured God as a lumberjack chopping down the tall trees. But who are the tall trees? They could refer to Jerusalem's leaders as they contemplate joining the rebellion. They could refer to the approaching Assyrian army. The prophet said in effect, "If the shoe fits, wear it, and suffer the consequences."

The Spirit's stump of salvation (11:1-9).—*700 BC(?), Ironical use of prophetic coronation oracle.* At some time within his ministry, Isaiah lost all hope for the present kingship. This could have been during the crisis with Ahaz in 733 BC or again with Hezekiah in 713 BC or 701 BC. Perhaps during an actual coronation ceremony or at a festival celebrating the role of the king, Isaiah stepped up to perform the traditional prophetic role of announcing God's blessing and legitimation of the king (compare Ps. 2). His first words shocked the audience. He did not speak of a Davidic king. He did not refer to the present king. Instead, he pointed to a coming king from the stump of Jesse, a branch growing out of roots. He presupposed that the present line of Davidic kings was dead. This agrees with the thought of Isaiah's contemporary Micah, who sent Judah back to Bethlehem for a new king (Mic. 5:2). Samuel's search in 1 Samuel 16 would have to be repeated. Israel needed a new kind of king, one filled with the Spirit like David (1 Sam. 16:13; compare 1 Sam. 10:6,10; 11:6; 16:14,23; 18:10; 19:9,23).

The prophet no longer used military imagery to describe the king (as in ch. 9). He turned, instead, to the language of the wise men, the court counselors. The divine Spirit would reveal itself in the king's spirit of wisdom, so that he could make proper plans and give proper advice and teaching. The center of such thought is the fear of the Lord, as often in wisdom thinking.

The wise king would enter the royal courtroom to judge his nation correctly. As judge, the king would be empowered with "the breath of his lips," (v. 4) the same word translated "spirit" in verse 2. By this he would protect the poor from the wicked, establishing the economic justice so central to prophetic preaching. The new age established by the new king would bring righteousness, a dominant theme for Isaiah. Coupled with faithfulness, this clothed the king for his royal reign.

Such a king would not bring just a transformation of the social order. Nature, too, would be restored to paradise. Natural enemies would feed together. A lad would surpass even the wildest childhood dreams, becoming king of the jungle. Human power, alone, could not accomplish this. The holy mountain, where God resided, provided the center. From there, personal acquaintance with Yahweh, the God of Israel, would flood out over the entire world.

No Israelite king took Isaiah's role description for a proper king seriously. God did, however. Centuries later, when the Jews least expected it, the stump of Jesse blossomed into life once more. Jesus Christ, filled with the divine Spirit, came to minister to the poor and outcast of society, and to give his wise teachings to the world. Since that moment, the knowledge of God has gradually flowed through the world. The bold goal of letting all the world know of Jesus of Nazareth has not yet been reached, yet his church continues the mission of proclamation on which he sent them. One day he will return to realize fully the vision of Isaiah.

The day of decision (11:10-16).—*Prophecy of salvation.* Verses 10 and 11 are prose descriptions of the coming "Day of Yahweh" used to interpret and connect the two poetic oracles in 11:1-9 and 12-16 (compare 7:18-25). To do so, they took up the language of both oracles. The messianic king would function specifically for the nations, an idea only hinted at in verse 9. The holy mountain where God dwelt would entice the nations with its splendor and glory. Such an action of God can only be described as a second Exodus (vv. 11,15), a purchase or ransom of Israel from slavery (see Ex. 15:16; Ps. 74:2).

Pathros (v. 11) refers to southern Egypt south of Memphis (see Jer. 44:1,15). Elam is the land east of Babylon and the lower Tigris on the Persian Gulf. Its capital was at Susa. Shinar is an old name for Babylon. The coastlands of the sea probably refer to the Phoenician coast.

The salvation hope here includes both the Northern and Southern Kingdoms. The Northern Kingdom went into exile first in 732 BC and finally in 722 BC (2 Kings 17). The invasion of Sennacherib and Hezekiah's dependence upon Egyptian help (2 Kings 19) may have driven some Jews into exile in Egypt, but the major flight to Egypt came only in the Babylonian crisis of 609-587 BC (2 Kings 23:29 to 25:30). This oracle apparently looked to the time when both kingdoms lost their independence and would rely on Yahweh for a new miracle to recreate his people. Then he would raise his signal flag to the nations, who would allow God's people to return home. God would reunite the two parts of his people, jealousy and hostility disappearing. Israel would then conquer anew their neighbors to the east and west, restoring the Davidic kingdom (compare 2 Sam. 8). God's new Exodus (vv. 15-16; compare Ex. 14) would lead across a special highway laid from Assyria, where the Northern Kingdom was captive (2 Kings 17:6,23; 18:9-12). Similar language appears in the second half of Isaiah to describe the return of Judah from Babylon (Isa. 40:3; 49:11; 62:10; cf. 19:23).

The Remnant's Response (12:1-6)

Song of thanksgiving (See 9:1-7.) The prophetic disciples who collected Isaiah's preaching (see 8:16) marked the end of the first collection of sermons with a song which should be sung "in that day," that is when the prophecy found its fulfillment, when the remnant of God's people had returned to their land from foreign exile. The first twelve chapters were thus prepared for use in the worship of the post-Exilic community.

The opening verse of the song startles the reader, reading literally, "I thank you, O Yahweh, because you were angry with me" (AT). This is modified to describe God's turning, his repentance of his anger, to console his people. The song was placed in the first person singular to make it personal. Reflecting upon one's personal history, the believer praised God for the time of discipline and for the deliverance from that crisis period. Having expressed gratitude, he then turned to traditional language of praise to describe the greatness of God in his relationship to the individual believer (compare Ps. 118; Ex. 15).

Verse 3 turns from the individual you of verse 1 to the plural you of the entire congregation. The great salvation of God was not confined to the individual, but encompassed the entire congregation. Everybody must join the hymn of praise (v. 4). The individual congregation is not large enough. Praise must echo throughout the entire earth (vv. 4-5). Such praise should resound to distant nations, inviting them to join the proclamation. Dark overtones cloud Isaiah 1—12, but the remnant's rousing response rings it to a close. Salvation is God's final word for his people. The Holy One of Israel resides in his Temple in Zion, the center of his praise.

Punishment for the Peoples
13:1 to 23:18

The Israelite prophet often counseled the nation and its leaders in times of political crisis. In time of battle the prophet reassured the army with an oracle promising victory against the enemy (see 1 Kings 20:28; 1 Sam. 15:2-3). This was another custom which Israel shared with her neighbors (Num. 22—24). Preaching against the enemies was not limited to times of battle. Times of national weakness and crisis called the nation to the Temple for services of national mourning and grief. Prophets rose to announce the divine answer to the nation's prayers. Parts of such answers dealt with the enemies, who formed a large part of the cause of Israel's grief.

Amos transformed the tradition of preaching against the nations into a literary art form by listing several such sermons together and then suddenly including his own people in the oracles against foreign nations (Amos 1:3 to 2:16). We have seen how Isaiah used a similar device in 9:7 to 10:11. Most of the other prophets included such oracles against the enemies.

Sermons against the enemies dominate 13:1 to 23:18, but there are also sermons against Judah (ch. 22), including her as an enemy of

God. By this means, a section which should bring hope to the people of God was transformed into a judgment against sinners in general, no matter what their national origin. The sermons are more. They were directed against nations seeking political alliances with Judah. For Judah, they served as warnings against political alliance. Judah's only ally was her God.

Banishing Babylon (13:1 to 14:23)

About 570 BC, Call to battle. The Hebrew word for "oracle" is a technical term for a prophetic sermon and usually occurs in headings introducing books or oracles. Otherwise it occurs only in Proverbs 30:1; 31:1; 2 Kings 9:25; Lamentations 2:14; 2 Chronicles 24:27.

Babylon was the capital of ancient Babylonia between the Tigris and Euphrates rivers, south of modern Baghdad. In Isaiah's day it looked back to the glorious days of Hammurabi (1792-1750 BC) and a brief revival under Nebuchadnezzar I (1146-1123 BC), but was suffering impatiently under Assyrian rule. Isaiah himself saw Babylonian secret diplomacy trying to overthrow Assyrian rule (see ch. 39), but did not see Babylon as the "glory of kingdoms" (13:19). The historical context here is that of Babylon after the rise of Nabopolassar in 626 BC and after Nebuchadnezzar's destruction of Jerusalem in 587 BC, which established Babylon as Judah's enemy number one for all time.

The prophet mysteriously called an unnamed army to lift the battle insignia and prepare for war. The army was composed of Yahweh's specially consecrated warriors highlighting the awesome atmosphere. Divine anger dominated the scene. The commanding general was the divine Warrior (v. 4), the Lord of hosts. He did not immediately reveal the nature of the army being summoned, indicating only that it was "from a distant land, from the end of the heavens" (v. 5). Instead, he issued an invitation to a mourning ceremony because of the approaching "day of the Lord" (v. 6; see 2:12-22). This would strike terror in the enemy and throw the cosmos into confusion (vv. 7-10). Man's pride stood in the center of the divine attention (v. 11). The remnant would be as rare as gold (v. 12). The nations in exile would be able to flee home in the confusion (v. 14). The horrible atrocities of war would be commonplace (vv. 15-16).

Having created such a tense and gloomy atmosphere, the prophet finally introduced the cast of characters. The army summoned by God for his purposes is the Medes (v. 17), from northwest Iran with their capital at Ecbatana. They had settled the area about 1400 BC. They battled the Assyrians at least from 800 BC onward, but had to pay tribute to Assyrian kings at least from about 720 BC until king Cyaxares (ca. 625-585 BC) joined Babylon in defeating the Assyrians (612-610 BC). Cyrus, king of Persia, the son of a Median king, revolted against the Medes and destroyed their empire (553 BC). Isaiah 13 and 21 join Jeremiah 51 in picturing the Medes as God's historical agents used to bring the Day of Yahweh against Babylon in punishment for its treatment of Judah. Second Kings 17:6 and 18:11 show that some of the Israelite exiles went to Media.

God's agents could not be bribed (v. 17). They would treat Babylon just as she treated Judah with all the atrocities of war (v. 18). Finally, in verse 19, the prophet named God's enemy facing destruction—mighty Babylon.

Chaldeans (v. 19), a synonym for Babylon, referred originally to tribal groups in southern Babylon near the Persian Gulf. They gained political control of Babylon under their kings Nabopolassar and Nebuchadnezzar II and were responsible for the destruction of Jerusalem in 587 BC. Now, said the prophet, their time had come. Their city would become uninhabited wilderness (vv. 20-22).

Chapter 14 shows the effects of Babylon's destruction for Israel. Israel would again know God's compassion, his parental love for his children, which guaranteed the security of their lives. Through such love God forgave a repentant people and restored them to their land. Love is the opposite of divine anger which brought judgment. As such it represents the freedom of God in dealing with his people (Ex. 33:19). Such love thus belongs to the very nature of God himself.

Such love brings God to choose Israel *again*. Such election theology is unique to Israel among her neighbors in the Near East. It is first expressed in Deuteronomy 7:6-8. The response to such loving election is also made clear in Deuteronomy 10:12-16. Israel's refusal to obey brought the expected punishment (see Deut. 30). After punishment, God's love brought a renewed election, restoring Israel to her land for a second chance with God (compare Deut. 4:36-39). Now the definition of Israel was expanded, for the foreigners who lived in the land would join Israel. Israel's political power would again exert itself, turning the tables on her former captors.

Israel would again experience rest (v. 3), the goal of the original conquest (Ex. 33:14; Deut. 3:20; 12:10; 25:19; Josh. 1:13,15; 21:44; 22:4; 23:1).

Having received anew God's love, election, and rest, Israel would mock her enemies (vv. 4-20) as once they were mocked (see Ps. 137). She would be joined by the whole earth, which Babylon once ruled, but which now would have rest (v. 7). Even the trees and the realm of the dead (see Isa. 5:8-30) would join in, as Babylon in the person of her king was escorted to her eternal resting place to be greeted by former kings who had lost their power, too (vv. 8-12). This was all because of Babylon's pride, trying to occupy the throne of God (vv. 13-14). Now she did not even have a proper tomb (v. 19). The prophet concluded with a curse on Babylon (vv. 20-21), seeking to prevent a repetition of such pride and destruction. Anyone with a claim to inherit the throne would be destroyed (compare 1 Kings 15:29; 2 Kings 10:17). No longer should captive peoples such as Judah have to suffer under royal building projects seeking to glorify the king of Babylon. God confirmed that he would answer the prayer and bring the curse to reality (vv. 22-23).

Aiming at Assyria (14:24-27)

701 BC, Divine oath against the enemy. The divine Commander raised his hand to solemnly swear that Assyria, just as Babylon, would not have the last word in history. As Assyria had once been the "rod of my anger" (10:5), now God will not spare the rod on her. He had considered all the evidence and worked out his plan. His hand once stretched over the people of God (5:25; 9:12,17,21; 10:4) would now extend over Assyria. This would have universal effects, because Assyria controlled virtually the entire universe. Such a prophetic judgment went against all historical probability, for Sennacherib was already in the country on "my land," upon "my mountains" (v. 25). The prophet was convinced that the Lord of hosts had greater military might than any earthly general. His strength was not limited to Israel, but extended over all the universe.

Panic Among the Philistines (14:28-32)

725 BC, Invitation to mourning ceremony (see 13:6). The Philistines were the first major threat to Israel's independence (Judg. 14:16; 1 Sam. 4:7; 13—14; 17; 27—31). David finally defeated them (2 Sam. 5:17-25), but after the division of the monarchy (1 Kings 12), the Philistines again gained their independence and repeatedly threatened Israel and Judah. The Assyrians subdued the Philistines in 734 BC and again in 733 BC under Tiglath-pileser. At his death, the Philistines had every right to rejoice and look for better days ahead. Isaiah called them to come to the house of worship not for thanksgiving but for mourning. The worst was yet to come. On the northern horizon Assyria was already coming again. Indeed! The years ahead brought the downfall of Gaza (720 BC), Ashdod (711 BC), and Ekron (701 BC), the major Philistine cities.

Isaiah's word was not simply a judgment on Israel's first major enemy. With it he warned Judah not to join the Philistine foolishness and revolt against Assyria. As in chapter 7, the prophet claimed political action could not save God's people. The hope for God's people lay with her God, not with her neighbor. The prophet had an explicit message for Philistine messengers who encouraged Judah to join in revolt (v. 32). God's people had been afflicted both by outside enemies and by their own rulers. The faithful would no longer depend upon kings and military action. They would seek refuge and rest in God.

Mourning for Moab (15:1 to 16:14)

728 BC, Mourning rituals and prophecy of judgment for Moab. Moab blocked Israel's way as she entered East Jordan and prepared to cross the Jordan (Num. 22:1 to 24:25) and enticed Israel into false worship (Num. 25:1-5). They traced their ancestors back to Lot (Gen. 19:37), which was the reason Israel could not claim Moab as her own territory (Deut. 2:9). Still, Moabite opposition brought forth divine law forbidding Israel to allow the Moabites to participate in Israelite worship (Deut. 23:3-6). The two nations warred constantly. On the other hand, Judah had close ties to Moab, for

David's ancestors were Moabites (Ruth 1:4; 4:13-22; 1 Sam. 22:3-4).

In the final years of Tiglath-pileser of Assyria, nomads on the border of Moab apparently crossed over and destroyed several of the major cities in northern Moab (15:2-4). The Moabites went to their temples for national rites of grief and mourning (15:2-3). Fugitives fled as far south as possible (15:5-8). The prophet mimicked the Moabite mourning (15:5; 16:9,11), but his own word promised more trouble to come (15:9). Even the remnant would not escape.

The text of 16:1-5 has caused translators problems as far back as the earliest translation into Greek (compare KJV; NEB; RSV; TEV; NIV). The Hebrew text as it stands reads: "You all send a ram of the ruler of the land from Selah (or the rock) of the wilderness to the mountain of the daughter of Zion" (AT). Neither the land nor the ruler is named. Apparently, Moab is meant, for the king of Moab was famous for his flocks (2 Kings 3:4). The king was either in Selah, the capital of Edom, or in the rocky wilderness. The prophet advised the king to pay tribute to Jerusalem and ask for political refuge and asylum for himself and his fellow refugees there.

Apparently, in verse 2 the prophet turned to his Jerusalem audience and described the plight of the Moabites, then gave advice as to how Jerusalem should react in kindness to the fugitives (vv. 3-4a). The basis of such advice is outlined in verse 5. Isaiah's understanding of the role of the Judean king was expressed in 9:2-7 and 11:1-9 and repeated here. The king of Judah did not fill the role in Isaiah's day. Nor did any other king. The Christian church points to Jesus of Nazareth as the only fulfillment, yet we still must wait for the coming day of total fulfillment.

When the prophet pointed to Jerusalem's responsibility to help the fugitives, he did not neglect Moab's deserved punishment. Pride went before the fall. (See 9:9; 13:3,11,19; 14:11; 23:9; 25:11; 28:1,3.) Moab's punishment brought drought and death for the fertile fields. Instead of songs celebrating the harvest, Moab would hear the victory songs of enemy warriors. Moab's thanksgiving festival would become a service seeking deliverance from the enemy. Isaiah predicted that such prayers would not win the victory (16:12). Later (v. 13), a new situation presented new hopes for victory, but the prophet repeated the same song, second verse: the few scattered survivors could accomplish nothing.

For Isaiah, the future of Moab was certain. Destruction awaited. Any intrigue which Moab started was doomed. Jerusalem must not depend on her help in rebellion against Assyria. Rather, Jerusalem must remember the task of her own kingship and the promises God had given her. Later Jeremiah 48 took up the same message in almost the same wording. Judah and her kings refused to learn God's lesson.

Doom on Damascus (17:1-3)

733 BC, Prophecy of disaster on a foreign nation. In the midst of the Syro-Ephraimitic War (see chs. 7—8), the prophet predicted total defeat for the invading Syrian army from Damascus and its ally from Israel. He concluded ironically that the remnant of Syria would be as great as the glory of Israel, which had lost all its defenses. Only pasture for flocks would remain.

Journey's End for Jacob (17:4-14)

733 BC, Prophecies of disaster against a foreign nation. The emphasis of the chapter turns to Jacob, the Northern Kingdom. This part of the people of God had become just another foreign nation God must destroy (see 9:8 to 10:4). The remnant of Israel could be numbered on one hand just as could the few grains of berries left by poor people who gleaned the fields clean after the harvesters had finished (compare Lev. 19:9-10; 23:22; Ruth 2:2-23).

Such drastic action was required to turn Israel away from her own creations to her Creator (vv. 7-8). Her attention had been focused on the wrong worship places and the wrong kinds of worship. The Asherah (v. 8) was a Canaanite goddess of fertility taken over by Israel and worshiped through the symbol of a tree or a special wooden pole. The symbol itself was also called the Asherah. The rather unusual word used for altars of incense appears to refer to a special type of altar used only in Canaanite worship. God would conquer Israel just as he did the peoples who lived there before Israel's conquest, if this is the correct reading of the very difficult Hebrew text (see RSV note; NIV on v. 9).

The reason for punishment is clear (vv. 10-11). Israel had worshiped foreign gods, using worship practices involving planting special plants which could blossom forth in a day to show the power of the god. Such worship magic would not help when God made the harvest flee like wartime fugitives.

Finally, the prophet summarized his understanding of the foreign nations (vv. 12-14), by pronouncing a woe oracle ("ah" of v. 12; Hebrew "Woe"). The nations were sound and fury, signifying nothing. God would blow them away like the chaff taken off the grain. They would simply create a giant dust storm, vanishing in a day. This was applied directly to Isaiah's audience, the people of Judah. They were afraid (see 7:4) without cause. They needed to make no international alliances. They needed simply to trust God (see 7:9).

Eyes Toward Egypt (18:1 to 20:6)

Prophetic eyes turned south to the first enemy Israel ever defeated. In the Exodus from Egypt Israel learned the personal name of her God—Yahweh (Ex. 3:13-16); experienced the power of her God among the nations (Ex. 14); learned how to worship her God (Ex. 12—13); and expressed her faith in Yahweh (Ex. 14:31 to 15:21). Centuries later historical fortunes had changed radically. The dominant world power was Assyria, not Egypt. Now Egypt sought political maneuvers to protect herself and tried to entice Judah to revolt against Assyria and depend upon Egypt for military and economic aid. Throughout the series of political maneuvers, Isaiah offered the word of God to his Judean leaders. Several pieces of his advice are gathered together in chapters 18—20.

In the early years of Isaiah's ministry, Egypt was a country divided against itself, rival rulers reigning in Tanis, Leontopolis, Heracleopolis, Hermopolis, Sais, and Thebes. Finally, Ethiopian rulers began to come north about 730 BC and by 715 BC controlled the entire country. Israel tried to make political alliances with Egypt against Assyria in 725 BC (2 Kings 17:4), resulting in the final destruction of the Northern Kingdom. In 720 BC Egypt tried to help Gaza, without success. In 716 BC Sargon II marched to the Egyptian border and received tribute from the king of Tanis. The Ashdod revolution of 712 BC brought Sargon back to Philistia, but the Egyptian king refused asylum for the Philistine ruler, giving him to Sargon. During

Sennacherib's expedition to Palestine in 702-701 BC in which Judah was devastated and Jerusalem besieged (see ch. 36), the new Egyptian king marched north to help but retreated quickly.

The Ethiopian pharaohs ruling Egypt sent a political delegation to Jerusalem either in 712 or 702 BC to conspire against Assyria. Isaiah responded with a woe oracle against them (18:1-7) predicting their destruction and calling on the leaders of Judah to trust in the word of God rather than the weak promises of Egypt. He promised, if his advice were followed, that Egypt would soon send another delegation to Jerusalem with offerings for the Temple.

Already in 716 BC Isaiah had warned against seeking Egyptian help (ch. 19). As in the Exodus, God himself would go to Egypt to defeat Israel's enemies. His presence would send Egyptian gods into panic (19:1). Internal revolution would shake the land. Egypt, noted of old for its wisdom, would find its plans confused and of no help (v. 3). God himself would give victory to a king who would rule Egypt harshly. It is not clear if Isaiah referred to a foreign king, such as the Assyrians, or to the new winner in the Egyptian revolution. The economic life of the land with its utter dependence upon the Nile would be destroyed, the river being totally dried up. Agriculture, weaving, and fishing would vanish. The entire work force would go into mourning (vv. 5-10).

Zoan (or Tanis) was the political center nearest Palestine. God had turned its counselors and rulers into fools (v. 11). They could not proclaim the purposes of the Lord of hosts, the God of Israel. Only the prophet could do that. Memphis was yet another center in northern Egypt (v. 13). Yahweh confused her wise men just like those of her northern competitor. Egypt had a horrible drunken hangover and was incapable of action (vv. 14-15).

The prophetic poetry turns to prose in vv. 16-25 giving explicit interpretation to the poetic oracle of 1-15. The mere mention of Judah would bring terror to Egypt because of the reputation of her God (v. 17). Five Egyptian cities would go so far as to learn the language spoken in Palestine, including Heliopolis, the "City of the Sun," if this is the right translation of a difficult Hebrew text (compare NIV) (v. 18). Verse 19 goes even further. An altar would be built in Egypt. This went against the grain of all Judean thinking. An altar belonged in Jerusalem and only in Jerusalem. What is more, a pillar was to be constructed.

In its earliest days Israel built memorial pillars at sacred spots.

The law prohibited such objects as part of worship since they were connected with Canaanite idol worship. Jeremiah 43:13 connected pillars (translated "obelisks" in RSV) with Egyptian worship at Heliopolis. Isaiah put a new face on the worship of Yahweh, permitting worship places in a foreign land.

Such worship would be a witness to the Egyptians. Yahweh must not be a holy terror for them (see v. 17), but can be their Savior, as he was Israel's Savior from the land of Egypt so long ago (v. 20; compare Ex. 3:9-10; 14:10-14). No longer must Israel escape Egypt to sacrifice to God (Ex. 5:1-3). The Egyptians would now sacrifice with them (v. 21). God introduced himself to Moses (Ex. 6:3) and tried to introduce himself to Pharaoh in the time of the Exodus (Ex. 5:2; 7:5,17; 8:10,22; 9:14,29; 11:7; 14:4,18). The prophet looked to the day when Egypt would truly know Yahweh (v. 21). Egypt's defeat would be her victory, for it would bring her to God to be healed (v. 22) rather than be plagued as in the Exodus.

The climax of the prophetic interpretation comes in verses 23-25. God would create a great triangle of nations serving him—Egypt, Assyria, and Israel (see 2:2-4). Highways would no longer echo the tramping of warriors but rather the trumpeting of worshipers. Finally, the promise to Abraham that his descendants will be a blessing to the nations can be fulfilled.

In 712 BC when Ashdod revolted, Judah was tempted once more to join in, expecting Egyptian assistance. Isaiah went to the extreme to get the political leaders of Jerusalem to listen to him (ch. 20). At the divine command, he performed a symbolic act. The prophet took off his clothes to appear as a prisoner of war marching into exile, symbolizing what would happen to Egypt with its new Ethiopian rulers. This would have great effect in Judah, which hoped Egypt would support the revolt. Apparently, Isaiah won the day, for Judah did not become involved in the Ashdod revolt, or at least withdrew in time to escape punishment from the Assyrian king.

Blowing Away Babylon (21:1-10)

701 BC, Awesome vision against Babylon. Babylon was the leader of intrigue against Assyria. Later she became the world power which destroyed Jerusalem in 586 BC. The prophetic oracle against

Babylon gained its title in an unusual fashion. The title (v. 1) does not describe the enemy, but the nature of the prophetic vision. The vision came from the wilderness of the sea (compare Ex. 13:18). God often came from the southern wilderness, from the holy mountain, to speak to his people (Deut. 33:2; Judg. 5:4; 1 Kings 19:8). The vision is grim (NEB), telling of the plunder and destruction of war (v. 2). Elam and Media are the attackers, but who is attacked? A people who have caused the world to groan (NIV)! The prophet hurried on, almost as if he were commenting on a set of slides flashing quickly on the screen. He described his own reaction (vv. 3-4). Unlike false prophets who gleefully played to the audience and rejoiced over the defeat of the enemy, he suffered agony that such horrors must enter the world. He was agitated, terrified (v. 3, NIV; KJV), and condemned to a sleepless night (v. 4). The scene changed to the generals enjoying a great banquet (v. 5), when they were called to battle. But whose generals? Next we hear God's command to set up a lookout for news of battle (vv. 6-7; see NIV, NEB). The lookout takes his post (v. 8) and finally spies the returning army (v. 9). The report of battle comes! Babylon is defeated. Her grand gods are ground to gravel. The prophet turned finally to his audience, addressing Judah as a people who have suffered enough of the horrors of war. He swore to tell the truth and the whole truth as God had shown it to him. He left his audience to draw the conclusions. Could Judah really depend upon Babylon and her gods in the fight with Assyria? Or should she return to trust in her own God who can predict the future?

Arrows over Arabia (21:11-17)

From 738 BC onward Assyria repeatedly forced the tribes and towns in the Arabian desert to pay taxes and recognize the authority of the Assyrian king. Again and again the tribes tried to regain their independence, but without success. Nabonidus, the last king of Babylon, spent ten years in Tema, about 550-540 BC. The nomadic tribes of Kedar finally established control over a large part of the Arabian desert around 500 BC, reaching possibly to the border of Judah and perhaps to Egypt. Their economic power exceeded their military might, for they controlled rich trade routes, delivering gold, precious stones, incense, and animals to their nothern trading partners.

Judah had particular interest in the rebellions of the Arabs. They indicated Judah's chances for success in similar ventures. Thus the prophet addressed three brief statements to the Arabians. The headings of the first two are difficult to understand. The first (v. 11) is against Dumah, which has been variously interpreted as the land of Edom, an Edomite city, an Arabian oasis, or simply a common noun "silence." The whole section seems to point to the Arabian town at the northern fork of the trade routes (compare Gen. 25:14 and 1 Chron. 1:30).

The content of the oracle shows that a word play on the meaning of "silence" is also intended. The prophet took the role of a night watchman on military guard duty. He heard an inquiry from across the southern border in Seir, another name for Edom. The watchman had no news, telling the inquirer to call back later. Silence from Arabia meant no time for Judah to revolt against Assyria. But action could come at any time. Stay tuned.

Action did come from Arabia. Verse 13 introduces a second oracle whose heading is not clear. The Hebrew term "Arabia" (RSV) occurs twice in this verse. Words very similar in sound mean *desert* or *wilderness,* and *evening.* Both have been suggested for the meaning here. The earliest Greek translation did not even translate the opening "the oracle concerning Arabia" and translated the second occurrence of the word "in the evening." The content of the oracle shows that the location is Arabia whether the heading actually referred to Arabia or not.

Dedan and Tema were oases south of Dumah in the Arabian desert. The prophet called upon Tema to help her neighbors who had been stranded in the desert after their trading caravan had been attacked. A people who cannot protect their own caravans certainly could offer no hope in a rebellion against a super power.

The Arabian section ends (vv. 16-17) with a prediction of disaster for the nomadic sons of Kedar. Arabs to the south provided no reason for hope for Judah in her rebellious ambitions against her Assyrian overlord to the east. Isaiah consistently told Judah to sit tight and wait for God's action, since military allies were not available and could not prevail.

Zion's Zero Hour (22:1-25)

701 BC, Oracle against the foreign nation Judah. This may be the last oracle preserved from the preaching of Isaiah. He had experienced the desperate situation of 701 BC (see chs. 36—39) and found no following. Here he described what occurred. When God won the victory over Assyria, forcing her to withdraw from Jerusalem, the people went into exultant jubilation. Fasting vanished. Feasting flourished (1-2a,13).

Isaiah looked deeper into the people's situation. The time of trial had revealed treachery. Leaders had deserted their posts to save their own necks, but were the only ones to lose them. God protected the city and those who remained faithfully at their post (2b-3). The lack of faith in Yahweh grieved the prophet beyond comfort (4). He recalled the scene. Assyria and her allies camped in the valleys surrounding Jerusalem. Particular emphasis is placed on "the valley of vision" (v. 5), probably referring ironically to prophetic visions reported in the valley of Hinnom outside Jerusalem (Josh. 15:8; 18:16). Such prophets would speak in the name of dead sons offered in sacrifice to foreign gods (2 Kings 23:10; Jer. 7:31-32; 19:2-6; 32:35). Isaiah said the true vision belongs only to Yahweh and his prophets.

Judah's lack of faith had produced the ominous day of Yahweh (v. 5; cf. 2:12), when God used enemy armies to judge Judah. Judah did not understand it so. She did not look to her God but to her special storehouse of weapons (v. 8; compare 1 Kings 10:17). She sought to man the barricades and repair the defenses at the last minute. It was too late for human effort. Only divine effort could bring deliverance (Isa. 37:36-38). Israel's creator certainly had power to protect and preserve (v. 11).

In the midst of Israel's victory celebrations a new word came from God. Mourning and weeping, not merriment and wantonness, was the order of the day! (v. 12). Why? Because neither in the midst of crises nor in the moment of miracle did Judah learn her lesson. She just would not turn in trust to her God. She refused to repent. So the prophet took up the proverb (13b) to counsel the folk to go blindly on with their celebration. Others would mourn their death tomorrow. Verse 14 summarizes the message dramatically and emphatically, with the divine oracle formula at its beginning and end. God swore an oath against Judah. The people who would not take his advice and thus had to face agony and destruction had been given a final chance to repent. Instead they celebrated the success of their own powers. They would have to face agony and destruction.

This was demonstrated not only on the national level, but also on the individual. Shebna, the chief official in charge of the king's house, proudly used his office to gain glory and eternal fame for himself. God moved in to whirl him into a distant land where he could not even use his burial chamber (v. 19).

The prophet used the language of the ceremony of installation in office to announce Shebna's successor—Eliakim (see 2 Kings 18:18,26,37; 19:2; Isa. 36:3,11,22; 37:2). The prophet had high hopes, calling him the servant of God (v. 20). The Old Testament seldom uses "servant of God" for a lower official.

Sadly, Eliakim proved no better. He could not bear the weight of his own family, who apparently demanded high positions at court for themselves (v. 24). So Eliakim had to be taken down a peg.

Chapter 22 shows that collectively and individually Jerusalem had become just another of the enemies of Yahweh and was set for destruction. What a sad climax for the prophetic ministry! Only the power of God in inspiring a faithful remnant to preserve his message gave new life to that ministry and made it eternally valid.

Taps for Tyre (23:1-18)

704 BC (?), Call to mourning. The oracles against the nations do not end with Jerusalem. They turn finally to the far northeast, to Phoenicia. Israel had depended on Phoenicia for overseas trade since the very beginning of the monarchy (2 Sam. 5:11; 1 Kings 5:1). This was natural. The major political powers of the world—Babylon, Assyria, and particularly Egypt—depended on the Phoenician seamen to transport their exports over the known world. The Phoenicians had been plying the sailors' trade since 3000 BC. Dependence on the Phoenicians created economic problems for Israel (1 Kings 9:10-14). One way to solve such problems was marriage alliances (1 Kings 16:31), but this brought religious problems (1 Kings 16:32-33).

The major Phoenician city was Tyre, located on a rocky island off the coast forty-five miles southwest of Beirut and about thirty-five miles northeast of Haifa. Racially the people were part of the Canaanites (v. 11), but their political ties were with Egypt (vv. 3,5). They also established trading colonies far and wide from the nearby island of Cyprus (vv. 1,12), to Carthage on the African coast, to Tarshish, probably in Spain (vv. 1,6,10).

Despite their wealth and sea power, the Phoenicians could not remain politically independent. As early as 858 BC they paid tribute to Shalmanezer III of Assyria. Generally they were content to pay tribute, but occasionally, they rebelled. We know of Tyre's participation in revolts against Assyria in 734-723 BC (when Tyre was besieged for five years), 704-701 BC (when Tyre apparently lost most of her control over Phoenicia), 676 BC (when Sidon was destroyed), 671 BC, and 663 BC. Isaiah 23 apparently involves the participation of Tyre in the major revolt of 704 BC (see chs. 36—39), in which Tyre was defeated and its king forced to flee to Cyprus.

Isaiah pictured Phoenician sailors returning home from a trading expedition. They heard the news of defeat as they came to Cyprus (v. 1), and the prophet called them to mourn. The result of the catastrophe is described in a speech of the sea, Phoenicia's source of income (v. 4). The sea complains that she is not productive. The mourning spread to the chief trading partner Egypt (v. 5), as well as Tarshish, possibly representing the geographical extremities of the Phoenician shipping routes.

Tyre had become unrecognizable (v. 7). The major question was "Who is powerful enough to accomplish this?" Could it be the king of Assyria? Of course not, only Yahweh the God of Israel had such power (vv. 8-9). The text, translation, and interpretation of v. 10 is very difficult (compare TEV, NIV, NEB, KJV). The only language which can describe the event (v. 11) is that of the act of God in the Exodus (Ex. 15:12; Deut. 4:34). The king might escape to Cyprus (v. 12), but it would do no good.

With verse 13 we again meet difficult problems of translation (compare RSV, NIV, TEV, NEB). The Hebrew refers to the Chaldeans, the people who took over Babylon in 626 BC. They besieged Tyre for thirteen years, beginning about 585 BC, and eventually sent the king of Tyre to Babylon in exile, marking the beginning of the end of Tyre as an international power.

A new linguistic image appears in verse 15. Tyre is pictured as an old harlot who has lost her charms and wanders forlornly through the city streets singing her charming songs trying to attract attention to herself without much luck. Such punishment must last seventy years, a round number used to express the lifetime of a generation (compare Ps. 90:10). Then Tyre would regain her harlot's charms and continue to earn her hire from strangers (v. 17). She would have a new master and bring her earnings to him at the Jerusalem Temple (v. 18). The people of God, not Egypt nor Assyria nor Babylon, would benefit from the Phoenician trade.

The oracle against Tyre served two functions. First, it joined the other oracles against the nations in warning Judah of any political alliances. Not even the island stronghold of Tyre was safe. She could certainly promise no help to Judah. Second, if Judah would wait, God would give her victory in time. Then she could enjoy the spoils of Tyre for herself. Alas, Tyre fell, but Judah would not listen to God and also fell, never getting to enjoy the favors of Tyre.

Apocalyptic Announcements
24:1 to 27:13

Having described the weakness and hopelessness of the nations, the Book now draws theological conclusions. What will this mean for the world as a whole? What will it mean for the people of God? How does God want his people to respond? Has hope vanished for everyone?

Cosmic Convulsions (24:1-13)

Prophecy of disaster against the earth. This section sets the stage for what follows and summarizes what has preceded. Add up the message of chapters 13—23, and you get one answer: total disaster on the whole earth. No social or economic class is exempt (v. 2). Why? The whole earth stands guilty before God. They have broken his "everlasting covenant" (v. 5). Genesis 9:8-17 tells us that the "everlasting covenant" (v. 16) promised that God would not repeat the destruction of the days of Noah. Isaiah 24 shows that the eternal covenant included laws and statutes which the whole world should understand and obey. When the whole world neglects the self-evident moral rules of the universe, God is bound to bring devastating punishment. Covenant curses must follow (compare Deut. 27:11-26; 28:15-68). Rejoicing was rejected; parties perished. Desolation dominated.

Reason to Rejoice? (24:14-23)

Prophetic argument. Hearing the prophecy of disaster for the earth, the people of God break into songs of praise. Time to worship and rejoice! Exiles from all corners of the globe join in. Jerusalem's day had come. The prophet reacted violently (v. 16). He returned to mourning. It was not yet time to rejoice. Even the people of God had not learned their lessons. Treachery, not truthfulness, reigned. The announcement of judgement must be repeated (vv. 17-20); the earth "falls" because "transgression" has pulled it down (v. 20).

The prophet was not through. Judgment is not the final word. "That day" is coming (v. 21). Heavenly and earthly powers will fall. The divine Jailkeeper will throw them in prison to serve their justified sentence (v. 22). Moon and sun, elements worshiped by Israel's neighbors as the high gods of the universe, must hide their faces in shame before the brilliance of his Majesty, King Yahweh. He, who has been worshiped as king in Jerusalem (Pss. 93; 95—99), will reveal his kingship with his dazzling glory. As at the founding revelation at Sinai (Ex. 24), so now the elders of God's people would be present. The glory which Isaiah discovered in his call vision (ch. 6) would become visible finally to the whole earth. Sadly, total judgment had to bring the earth to its knees before they could see his majesty. Sad also that the people of God are so quick to leap into action with their songs of rejoicing while God is still punishing the earth for its stubborn sinfulness. The prophet said for them to mourn for the sad state of the world until that day when God chooses to reveal his glory.

Sing to the Savior (25:1-12)

Hymn of Thanksgiving (see ch. 12). When God has ascended the divine throne before all the earth, thanksgiving and rejoicing will be in order. The prophet even provides the right hymn. Thanksgiving is addressed to "my God," being based on a personal relationship, not hearsay evidence. Normally God is praised for his wonderful deeds (Ex. 15:11; Isa. 29:14; Ps. 77:11,14). Here the focus is moved into the future. The prophet praises God for planning to bring to pass deeds which can be compared only to the great wonders of salvation history (compare 9:5). Such plans are "faithful and sure" (v. 1). "Formed of old" (v. 1) should probably be translated "from afar." The deeds are described as the destruction of "the city" (v. 2), to be understood as the capital of the great enemy, left unnamed. The results are astonishing; the defeated enemy turns to worship Yahweh. The result for God's poor people is peace. Certainly, this is an appropriate thanksgiving to follow the events of chapter 24.

Thanksgiving is not only sung but also is acted out in a meal celebrating God's kingship, a meal open to all nations (vv. 6-7). No longer will the nations veil themselves in mourning over the victims lost in the battle of the last days. God will invite all who are left to feasting and joy together. Death, the last enemy, will be conquered (v. 8). Thus the people of God again break out in thanksgiving (v. 9).

The chapter ends by naming Moab as the enemy and describing its fate (vv. 10-12; compare chs. 15—16).

Praise for the Promise of Peace (26:1-21)

Again a proper response is given the people. This song should be sung when they join the victory procession into Jerusalem after God has given the final victory. Victory is reserved for the righteous nation which keeps faith (see 3:10; 11:5), the people who trust in God (see 12:2). Such trust must not be fleeting. It must endure forever (v. 4). God responds to such trust with victory for his poor ones (vv. 5-6). They can use familiar proverbs to repeat their confession of trust in their God (v. 7).

The people of God should not remain content with singing about the victory to come. They should also bring the brutal facts of present reality to God (vv. 8-18). Here is the language of lamentation known so well from the Psalms. In time of trouble, God's people pleaded with God to act so that the wicked would learn their lesson (vv. 9-11). They confessed their confidence that God would bring peace (v. 12). They claimed their innocence despite overwhelming temptations (v. 13). They called to mind the great deeds of God for them in the past (vv. 14-15), wherein their enemies were totally wiped out. They described their own distress and helplessness (vv. 16-18). The last line of verse 18 should probably be translated "and no one will be born to inhabit the world" (NEB).

God heard and answered (v. 19). Many interpretations of his answer have been given. The Hebrew text reads, "Your (singular) dead ones will live; my corpse they will rise. Awake and rejoice you dwellers in the dust, for the dew of the lights is your (singular) dew, but the land of the Rephaim will cause to fall" (AT). The early interpreters from the Dead Sea Scrolls on had trouble interpreting this verse and translating it. Before studying the text, you will do well to read several modern translations. The verse repeats in some way the promise of victory over death given in 25:8. It stands in stark contrast to the fate of Israel's former enemies (v. 14). This verse may mean simply that in contrast to the enemies, the nation of Israel will live again, being able to produce children instead of being barren, as she was pictured in verse 18.

The agricultural image of the last half of the verse referring to the dew which was all important for Israel's agricultural hopes may simply be a promise of renewed growth of crops in a dead land. However, the context apparently demands something more than this. The horrible, barren situation of God's people in the last days (compare 24:16-23) can be changed only by something revolution-arily new. We have here the "earliest reference in the Bible to the resurrection" (Page H. Kelley, *Broadman Bible Commentary* © 1971 Broadman Press, Vol. V, 267).

Such hope is not immediate, however. God's people must wait. For the period of waiting, God gives directions: hide quickly! (v. 20). Why? Because God's uplifted hand will no longer be hidden (v. 11). Indeed, the earth will receive its punishment (v. 21). Murder can no longer be concealed. God will revenge his innocent followers. But until he does, his people must hide and wait, preparing to join in the victory procession of peace.

Ready for Renewal and Revenge (27:1-13)

The judgment against the nations and the view towards the last days climaxes in a statement ranging from creation to the final day of salvation. It begins by taking up ancient language of a battle at creation between God and Leviathan, the chaos monster (see Ps. 74:14; 104:26; Job 3:8; 41:1). The day is coming when the powers of darkness and chaos will hold no fear for God's people. God has been in control since the world began and will finally prove this once and for all "in that day" (vv. 1-2,12).

The new day will be a day of total transformation. Even the prophetic message will be transformed. The "Song of the Vineyard" of Isaiah 5:1-7 can no longer be sung in judgment of Israel (vv. 2-6). God will sing the song in praise of his vineyard. His anger will disappear (v. 4). He will protect rather than destroy his vineyard. He wants everyone, even the enemy, to come to him and grasp hold for peace and protection, just as people had at one time run to his Temple and grasped the horns of the altar for safety (1 Kings 1:50; 2:28). The vineyard of God will prosper and provide good fruit for the whole universe (v. 6; compare 5:7).

Such hope for God's people is not automatic. God lays requirements on his people. This is the message of verses 7-11, though the precise translation and interpretation is difficult, especially in verse 8 (TEV is probably right here). God has punished his people, but not as severely as he has their enemies (v. 8).

If Israel wants God's final blessing and peace, she must respond to the punishment of God and remove the altars and other paraphernalia she has used to worship false gods (v. 9). Otherwise, Israel would be forced to remain content with what she had, a deserted city with a great past and no future (v. 10). Even in an apocalyptic promise of the final salvation for God's people, demands are made on God's people. No salvation of God is automatic. A people who have no understanding, no thought for God, cannot simply wait until God decides to exercise his great compassion and grace. The Creator looks to the day when he can destroy the powers of evil and chaos forever, but he waits for the day his people are discerning and reject the sins which have caused their punishment.

When that day comes, God will sound forth his trumpet to call all his people back from their exile in the east and west. God's people will no longer worship other gods. They will join together in God's chosen place to worship the Holy One of Israel on his holy mountain (vv. 12-13). This is the ultimate goal of God for his people.

Mandate Against Military Might
28:1 to 39:8

The Assyrian section of the Book of Isaiah concludes with a series of prophetic sermons and narratives calling Judah to trust in her God for deliverance in all times of crises rather than to expect the military might of her government or of any allies to help her. This structure shows us that the apocalyptic hope for the last days when all the national enemies are defeated is not the last word of the prophet. Such hope is the reason for God's people to trust him and his ways in the midst of present crisis.

Doom for the Dumb Drunkards (28:1-13)

724 BC, Woe oracle. The Northern Kingdom lost most of its property and its hope for independence in 732 BC, but hope sprang eternal in the Ephraimite breast. King Hoshea refused to pay tribute (2 Kings 17:4). Isaiah described the stupidity of such a proud act by describing the drunken parties being celebrated in Samaria, the northern capital. Such parties may well have taken place at the Temple (compare Ezek. 23:36-45). Isaiah quickly turned the woe against the party goers to a description of Assyria's reaction (vv. 2-4). Samaria with her defense wall sat like a proud crown on a hill overlooking the valleys below. She would become nothing more than the fading flowers worn like a crown by the party goers. Certainly the one who wore the crown of Samaria must have sensed that he had not been forgotten by the prophet.

The true crown bearer was the only hope to crown his people with beauty. The sad truth was that only a remnant would remain to receive the crown (v. 5). They would receive a new ruler who would be controlled by the "spirit of justice" rather than the spirits which flowed through the veins of the ruler of Isaiah's day. This new ruler would then win any battle, even if the enemy had already entered the city gates (v. 6).

The royal party was not the only culprit. Religious leaders who were supposed to seek the word of God and give it to the people could not blame an ecstatic experience of the Spirit for their condition. They had imbibed of other spirits (vv. 7-8). Religious parties rather than prophecies ruled their days. (Compare Lev. 10:8.) Isaiah shows us here that the Temple staff included both priests and prophets whose job it was to teach the people of God and to interpret messages God sent to his people (see Deut. 17:8-12). In such festive conditions they could not accomplish the assigned task. God was left with babies, or with adults whose action (v. 8) was no better than babies, to instruct and direct his people.

The priests and prophets did not take the insult from Isaiah lying down. They shouted back, trying to mimic Isaiah and accuse him of saying one thing on one occasion and another at a different time— one time judgment, another time hope. They would see themselves as consistently promising hope for God's people. We must admit that the precise translation and explanation of verse 10 is not clear (compare RSV, NEB, TEV, and especially NIV and its note).

God could no longer use the professional ministers. He had to call on foreigners who could speak the only language God's people appeared to understand, the language of military power (v. 11). God had tried to give his people rest, but they turned deaf ears to him (v. 12). God would fulfill his threat of judgment with the judgment threatened in 8:15, which is quoted here (v. 13), and all because God's ministers mixed drinks with their messages.

A Stone for the Scoffers (28:14-22)

733 BC, Prophecy of disaster. The dating and interpretation of this oracle are difficult. It appears that after Ahaz refused to take his advice (see 7:1-9), Isaiah turned to the king's political advisers and warned them of the consequences of their new political alliance with Assyria. Isaiah addressed these wise counselors with their own wisdom language, making plays on each Hebrew word. The "ruler" (v. 14, AT) also can mean "maker of proverbs." "Covenant with death" (v. 15) could be a ritual with a foreign god of the underworld, an alliance to fight to the death, or a treaty with a foreign power. The lies and falsehood could refer to the politicians' clever ability to make a treaty when it was useful with the clear intention to break it when it was no longer to their advantage. They could also refer to the worship of false gods. The foundation stone (v. 16) appears to refer either to the Temple, to a new king, or to a new building project which would ensure the defenses of the city. For the prophet, it becomes a stone of testing (not a "tested stone").

The prophet called the politicians away from rejoicing over their latest political achievement to remind them of the call for faith (7:9) made by God. The Master Carpenter was coming to the city. He was not in a building mood. Rather, he wanted to check out the security of the city. Had it been built straight and plumb? The tools of the Carpenter are justice and righteousness. The proper response is faith (v. 16) not fast action. Everything was out of plumb. The Master Builder would hail down stones from heaven to destroy what they had built. Their treaty partner would bring death and destruction. The Divine Warrior of 2 Samuel 5:20 and Joshua 10 would turn his powers against proud politicians. This would be a strange, foreign work of Yahweh (v. 21).

The politicians paid no attention. Sennacherib came and destroyed the whole land (see chs. 36—39). The word of God continued to speak to God's people. In the fullness of God's time a carpenter appeared in Galilee calling men to follow in faith his way instead of that of the political and religious leaders of his day. He became God's foundation stone by which even Gentiles gained righteousness through faith. He also became a stumbling stone by which the nonbelieving people of God found themselves tested and found wanting (Rom. 9:30-33; 10:11; 1 Pet. 2:6).

Facts from the Farmer (28:23-29)

701 BC (?), Prophetic instruction. In forty years of prophetic ministry, Isaiah faced many situations and found God's specific word for each situation. The people of Jerusalem, and even his own disciples, did not always understand what the prophet was up to. How could he proclaim oracles of judgment against Judah's enemies, and then turn around and say those enemies would be used to punish Judah? How could he proclaim that God was using Assyria to punish Judah, and then proclaim salvation for Jerusalem even when the Assyrian armies surrounded the city? Was God constantly changing his mind? Was God inconsistent in his actions?

At some point in his ministry, Isaiah took time to teach his disciples what he meant. To do so he borrowed the style and vocabulary of the wise men of Judah. He took up one of their parables and gave his own explanation. God could be compared to a farmer who engaged in many activities to prepare the ground, sow the seed, harvest, and thresh the crop. The farmer did not spend all his time doing the same thing. He did not act in the same way with the small spices and seasonings as he did with the larger grain crops. Yes, the farmer could be charged with inconsistency. The fact could not be denied. But he successfully produced his crops. Why? Because he used his God-given wisdom.

How much more wonderful was the wisdom of God himself in working to produce the proper fruit in his own people. God, too, did everything necessary at the proper time to bring forth the proper results. God could not be programmed and predicted by a computer. The ways of God were not determined once and for all in such a way that men could expect the same type of treatment constantly. Just as a farmer carefully watched his crops and did what was needed at each stage of growth, so God carefully watched his people and reacted personally to bring his people to be what he had created them to be. God was not programmable; he was personal. His works were not to be predicted, but to be praised! Other prophets might be consistent in their understanding of God's politics. Isaiah was consistent in his understanding of God's purpose.

Agony for Ariel (29:1-8)

701 BC, Woe oracle and promise of salvation. As the Assyrian army approached Jerusalem (see chs. 36—39), the people continued life as usual with their annual religious feasts (see Ex. 23:14-17). Isaiah promptly pronounced woe on such activities and attitudes. Note that "Ho" of verse 1 should be translated "Woe" (KJV, NIV). To show where the center of his interest lay, the prophet used the language of festival. "Ariel" is the top of the altar, the part on which sacrifices were burned (Ezek. 43:15-16). Jerusalem, the city taken by David (2 Sam. 5:7), could be compared only to the smoking altar, which did not itself burn but which caused everything around it to burn.

The city with the proud past and perverse present faced a fearful future full of mourning. The enemy would soon surround her walls. The boastful people who thought God could never give his people into the hand of the enemy would hide themselves in the ground and pretend to be dead to escape the enemy. They would be so scared they could only speak "like the voice of a ghost" (v. 4; see 8:19; 19:3). The enemy's teeming hordes would make the outlook hopeless.

Suddenly, the prophet changed the entire mood (v. 5). Beyond all expectations and hopes, in the midst of disaster and despair, God would intervene "in an instant." But what would God do? God's visitation (v. 6) is usually for judgment and punishment. The language of storm and fire sounds ominous. What would the multitude of nations (v. 7) do? Then the unexpected conclusion— they will vanish as a dream in the night! A specific historical example has proved correct the teaching of the preceding section. God's plans are neither programmed nor predictable. God is free to react to his people as he chooses. He can attack and punish his own people. He can just as suddenly turn the tables on his agent of discipline. God's people must respect the freedom of God and must seek to act in a way that is appropriate to the situation and is consistent with the word of God given to them for the situation.

The Ruin of Religion by Rote (29:9-16)

701 BC, Prophecy of disaster combined with woe oracle. In his call vision, Isaiah learned that his message would be ignored (6:9-10). His reaction was to plead for his people and ask "How long?" (6:11). Long years of ministry proved the truth of his first vision. In the crisis of 701 BC, Judah's politicians refused to listen to Isaiah's word from God, electing instead to depend upon Egypt and other allies in an attempt to gain independence from Assyria. Isaiah reacted by telling them to go ahead and continue in their retreat from reality. *Today's English Version* certainly has the proper sense in translating: "Go ahead and be stupid!" (v. 9). Here we see that the hardening of the people's hearts was related to a specific historical situation and began with the stupid actions and attitudes of the people. This was followed by the action of God. Instead of pouring out his spirit upon the prophets, God poured out a deep sleep, so deep the prophets no longer had visions. The people did not seek God's word from God's proper spokesman in God's proper time, so God would no longer provide even the opportunity to hear his word. Not only the living word to the prophets was closed. The written word in God's book was closed (v. 11) with no one able to open or read it.

The people themselves had an entirely different picture of things. They continued going to worship, singing hymns, and saying prayers (v. 13). The Temple was flourishing. But they were just doing what the priest taught them! They did not know God in personal experience. They expected nothing from him. Religion had become routine rather than real.

God promised to make it real. He would again do marvelous things. These miracles would not deliver Judah from political crisis. They would deliver the politicians from their burden of human wisdom which prevented their seeking divine wisdom.

In such a situation, facing new wonders of God, the prophet must again turn to his cry of "Woe!" Human wisdom had climbed upon the divine throne. Instead of asking God's advice, Judah's political counselors decided among themselves and then tried to hide their decision from God. They thought no one would know, so that no one could blame them if their plans failed. They might fool men. They could not hide from God. Their whole understanding was turned upside down. They were mere creatures. They could not tell the Creator what to do. They could not claim greater wisdom or power than God. Yet they tried! Woe!

Holy Help for the Humble (29:17-24)

725 BC (?), Promise of salvation. Stupidity and stupor were not the prophet's final expectations. A new day was coming. It may be that the coronation of Hezekiah brought new hope (compare 9:2-7; 11:1-9).

Even nature would mirror the hope. The cedar forests of Lebanon would be transformed into dense forests of fruit trees. The book (see v. 11) would be open, and the deaf could hear it read. The blind (see v. 9) would see. God's wonders would once more heal instead of wound his people. But the people would have a new image. No longer would proud politicians get rich off the weakness of the poor.

No longer would the legal processes of the court be turned to political and economic profit at the expense of the poor. In that day Yahweh would be the joy of the poor. When God's people accepted their identity as the poor ones depending on God rather than on human wisdom, then he would remove their shame (v. 22). The people then would react naturally by making the name of God holy (v. 23). Israel would trust God and the word of God's true prophet. They would give glory and honor to God for all his wonderful deeds rather than trying to gain credit for their own political wisdom. This is the foundation of the opening statement of the Lord's Prayer. Such an attitude represents a total reversal of the situation Isaiah described in 29:13-16. Finally the people would accept prophetic instruction (v. 24).

The Emptiness of Egyptian Embassies (30:1-7)

701 BC, Woe oracle. Chapters 18 to 20 did not deal sufficiently with the Egyptian problem. Isaiah had yet more to say. In a society which placed supreme value on children obeying their parents (Deut. 21:18-20), Judah had rebelled against their Heavenly Father. The rebellion is clearly defined. They trusted in a political alliance with Egypt rather than depending upon the word of God from his prophet. As always before, Egyptian help proved too little too late. Judah learned neither from her history nor her prophets. She continued to trust her political savvy. She continued to send political embassies to the various Egyptian cities (v. 4) seeking advice and military help. No one profited. Such help was worthless (v. 7). Judah wasted all her effort and resources seeking to carry treasures through the wilderness to entice Egypt to help her (v. 6). Egypt was as helpless as the chaos monster Yahweh killed at the creation of the world (v. 7b).

The Book that Brings Banishment (30:8-17)

701 BC, Prophecy of disaster. God had had enough. He had done all he could to prevent Hezekiah from rebelling against Assyria. Nothing he did worked. Finally, he told Isaiah to write his message down so that coming generations could interpret the inevitable disaster in light of what God had done. God could not be blamed for the destruction which Judah had to suffer. God's people had rebelled not only against Assyria; they had rebelled against him. He had sent seers and visionaries (v. 10, where the normal word for *prophet* is consciously avoided). They had refused to listen. Their preachers must only entertain them and give them hope. They did not want to hear of a Holy God, who demanded that his followers be a holy people (compare ch. 6). The people certainly found the kind of prophets they wanted (Isa. 9:15; 28:7; Mic. 3:5-8), but the words of such prophets did not prove true. They could not pass the test of time.

The sin of the people was like a small crack in a wall, unnoticed at first, but one day causing the wall to bulge out and fall suddenly. The resulting destruction would be so complete that it could be compared only to a potter who is so angry with his work that he smashes it to bits and then grinds them into the ground so that no recognizable piece remains. All is dust. In Isaiah's day, broken pots could still be useful to write messages, stir the coals of a fire, or even dip water (v. 14); but Judah's destruction would leave the nation so weak that it would be good for nothing.

Isaiah consistently called Judah to trust God in the most difficult political and military situations (compare ch. 7). Judah consistently trusted her political alliances, which Isaiah called "perverseness; . . . iniquity" (vv. 12-13). Isaiah trusted in the God who had proved his military might in the Exodus and the conquest. He called Judah to return and rest in this God who would give them strength for victory (v. 15). Judah wanted military cavalry like Egypt's and Assyria's (v. 16). Isaiah countered with the claim that such troops could not be trusted in the moment of crisis. They would flee at the first sign of trouble and leave Judah defenseless (v. 17). Judah refused to listen to Isaiah's word. He had to write it in a book to remind future generations that God banished those who believed in their own power instead of in God's.

Waiting to Wipe Away Weeping (30:18-26)

About 500 BC, Promise of salvation. The drastic judgment of the preceding section was not God's final word. The prophet knew the nature of God. He was just and gracious and merciful. As such he would restore the just order of the universe. This could come, however, only after the guilty have been justly punished. God's people must become a people in waiting (v. 18). This meant that the time for lamentation over the destruction of the Temple, such as appears in the Book of Lamentations, would pass (v. 19). God is a God who hears such complaints of his people and answers them with love and grace. Verse 19 provides all the reason necessary for God's people to pray to him in all honesty and depth of emotion as well as in total confidence and expectation of his answer in love and grace.

God punished his people to teach them the necessity of following him, but after the punishment God appeared again as the teacher present with his people to direct them along every step of the pathway of life (vv. 20-21). This meant that God's people should respond to the gracious guidance of God by removing from their midst anything which would lure them away from God (v. 22). The horrid nature of such things is shown in the Hebrew by describing them as "unclean things" (literally, menstrual discharge—see NIV) and then by making a word play using a term which means both "Begone" and "excrement" (see NEB).

God reacts to human obedience by showering his blessings. He promised that even the work animals would feast daily. Palestine, ever plagued by drought, would see water running from every hill. Such a paradise was tempered by the thought that not everyone would share in such blessings. The day of God's grace for his people would, at the same time, be a day of slaughter for God's enemies (v. 25). Those of his own people who were injured by God's punishment would find that God had become their Great Physician bandaging all their wounds. Weeping must come for God's disobedient people, but cannot be God's last word to his world.

Furious Festival of Fire (30:27-33)

701 BC, Divine theophany. Judah had experienced the great catastrophe of Sennacherib's destructive march through all her cities (see 36—39). Only Jerusalem remained. The prophet used traditional language to describe God's action in the moment of extreme crisis. The people thought God was afar off, having forgotten, but God would come from his holy residence to punish the nations afflicting his people. God controlled the nations just as a farmer controlled his beast of burden. Yahweh would lead these unruly beasts in the wrong direction as they tried to harm his people. Israel's lamentation would turn into a celebration of the holy festivals (contrast 24:14-16). Finally, in verse 31 we learn the cause of God's anger. Assyria, once the rod of God's anger (10:5), would now feel the brunt of his wrath.

The translation and interpretation of verses 32-33 are quite difficult, as a glance at several translations will witness. The "burning place" (v. 33) or oven involves a wordplay on the proper name Topheth (see NEB, NIV), the place where child sacrifice to pagan gods was practiced. The reference to the king again involves a wordplay promising judgment not only upon the king of Assyria but also upon Molech, the deity to whom child sacrifices were given. Now, said the prophet, God has prepared the sacrificial fire for the enemy and will light it himself. The fiery visit of God has burned the enemy but brought festive celebration to the people of God. Yet the people of God must remember that God's action can be understood only as an action of his grace (v. 18) upon a people whom he has had to punish severely. The people of Jerusalem forgot this and eventually called forth the horrible judgment of 22:12-14 upon themselves.

Human Helpers Humbled (31:1-3)

701 BC, Woe oracle. Assyria responded to the rebellions of 701 BC by entering Syria-Palestine with all her military power. She defeated the Philistines, even when Egypt tried to help by sending troops to Eltekeh. Then Assyria turned on Judah. Hezekiah and his political advisers continued to depend upon Egypt despite the evidence that she was powerless and despite Isaiah's continued warnings. In desperation, the prophet declared woe upon Egypt and those who sought help from her. He could not understand why God's leaders did not do the obvious thing and seek help from the Holy One of Israel. Certainly, the wisdom of Hezekiah's wise counselors could not be compared to that of God. Yet the king followed their foolishness rather than divine wisdom proclaimed by the prophet. Like Ahaz before him (ch. 7), Hezekiah could not believe and trust in God. The result was easy to predict. God would be faithful to his word of warning and defeat the plans of Hezekiah and his counselors. Planning and carrying out such counsel was just as big a sin as the sins listed in 1:12-17.

The basic sin was a false perspective. Judah placed Egypt in the place of God as the one who was all-powerful. Egypt claimed that her Pharaoh had divine powers. Isaiah claimed that only God had such powers. The outstretched divine hand still controlled Judah's military fate. The military power of Egypt and the wise counselors of Judah would perish together. The Holy One would either be Hezekiah's helper or humble his helpers.

Aid Against Assyria (31:4-9)

701 BC, Promise of salvation. Isaiah warned against all alliances with other nations. He condemned the political actions of Jerusalem's rulers. Still, at the final moment, when everything appeared hopeless, Isaiah had yet another surprise for his audience. He announced that despite the faithlessness of the people of God the Lord of hosts would prove himself faithful to his people. He would protect their capital. "Band of shepherds" (v. 4) is an appropriate wordplay, since kings were often called shepherds. God is pictured as a lion with his prey in his paws. The shepherds sought to scare him away from the prey. God remained strong and faithful to Jerusalem and would not forsake her. Such divine action should bring forth human repentance (v. 6). Repentance, in turn, should express itself concretely in the destruction of false gods and thus the total dependence upon Yahweh, the Lord of hosts. Politically, this meant that the Divine Warrior would raise his sword to strike down Assyria. God had a fire ready in Jerusalem to sacrifice the enemy who would attack the city (see 30:33).

Renovating Royalty (32:1-8)

700 BC, Messianic promise. The aged prophet looked back on a career replete with rejection. His high hopes for Hezekiah (see 9:2-7) lay hidden in history. His country was a shambles, only the capital remaining. Once more the prophet turned to God. Again a surprising word came forth. A new king remained the source of hope, one who would reign in righteousness, who would surround himself with princely advisers whose joy was justice. Storms, whether military or natural, would pose no threat. This king would set such an example that God's prophet would no longer face the deaf, blind audience among which Isaiah had labored so long (see 6:10; 29:9-10). Society would no longer be turned upside down (v. 5; compare 3:1-12). The land would no longer have foolish leaders bringing iniquity (see 31:2) and misinterpreting the word of God (see 30:9-11) while ignoring their social responsibilities and misusing their legal powers in the courtroom (see 29:21). The new king would be truly noble in what he planned and in what he rose to defend (v. 8).

Here is Isaiah's mature definition of kingship for Judah. Neither he nor his successors saw the ideal realized. In fact, Hezekiah's successor, Manasseh, proved to be just the opposite (2 Kings 21:1-16). In the fullness of time, God sent his Son to fill the role that the kings before him refused to fulfill. Even he had to call upon those who had ears to hear to listen. Yes, even the Messiah found the same deaf ears that confronted the prophet Isaiah.

Lazy Ladies, Lament! (32:9-14)

Call to lamentation. The prophet stood up as a teacher in front of his classroom and saw the girls acting silly and carefree. He called them to attention and warned them to take seriously the political situation of the day. It was no time for frivolity. Danger loomed on the horizon. It was time to cry and mourn before God in hopes that he would not let disaster happen. The terms "at ease" and "complacent" are not necessarily negative. The same Hebrew terms are used in verse 18 to refer to God's promise of a day when his people would live "in secure dwellings" and "in quiet resting places." The basic meaning of the terms is "security" and "trust." The question is the source of security and the time for trust. Jerusalem had come to the point of seeing her own political measures as the source of her security and "for ever" as the time for trust. The prophet had to teach the people that only God and his measures provided a source for security and that God brought his moment of discipline as well as the time for trust.

"In little more than a year" (v. 10) is an idiom whose meaning is not absolutely clear. It may mean simply, wait till next year, "when the year is out" (NEB), pointing ahead to the end of the harvest period when the new year was celebrated. The new year celebration would turn to mourning. Instead of harvest, the prophet predicted that God would bring destruction on a disobedient people. Only the beasts of the field would still have reason for joy. God's people must learn that they have "a time to weep and a time to laugh;/a time to mourn, and a time to dance" (Eccl. 3:4). The prophetic message found its fulfillment when the Babylonians completely destroyed the city of Jerusalem in 587 BC.

The Spirit Sows Salvation (32:15-20)

Promise of salvation. The chapter ends with a section tying back to the opening verses and promising salvation after the gruesome destruction of Jerusalem. Here we see how "for ever" (v. 17) can be limited in Hebraic thinking. God's gracious activity can rebuild even what gruesome human activity has totalled. This picture of salvation uses the language and images of verses 9-14 to show how God totally reverses things for his people. The passage also gives a climax to the hope expressed in chapters 9 and 11. Here is Isaiah's hope in a nutshell.

Such hope began with the spirit given by God. Commentators continue to argue whether the original text personified the spirit or not. The point is of little significance. God was acting from above to change radically the scene of people below. God's act would change life in both the physical and ethical realms. Fertility destroyed by the enemy (v. 10) would be multiplied so that fruit trees would grow as close together in the uninhabitable wilderness as trees in the natural forest. The wilderness dominated by the law of the jungle would be transformed into a human dwelling ruled by justice and righteousness. When conditions of justice and righteousness prevail among people, peace comes. Here is the prophet's major point which must not be missed. Peace, security, and trust among people can be achieved only when the Spirit of God rules to bring justice and righteousness among people. Only then will wars and rumors of wars cease. Only then can "My people" (v. 18) rightfully be "at ease in Zion" (Amos 6:1).

The meaning of verse 19 is hidden from us because the Hebrew text has not been well-preserved (compare KJV; TEV; RSV; NEB). Apparently, the text described the opposite pole of God's salvation, namely the judgment on the enemy city. In light of this, verse 20 turns to congratulate those who proved to be part of the people of God by pronouncing a blessing upon them. Both man and beast would be able to carry out their normal activities anywhere and everywhere they desired without any fear whatsoever.

Festival Against Foreign Foes (33:1-24)

Eschatological order of worship. As in chapters 12, 25 and 26, here the prophet provided an order of worship for the people of God who experienced God's salvation. This section is remarkable for the fact that the people of God do not recognize immediately that they are experiencing divine salvation. The section begins with a woe oracle against the unnamed enemy (v. 1), followed by the proper response of the people in lamentation (vv. 2-9), a prophetic oracle announcing divine judgment, again on an unnamed enemy (vv. 10-13), and a list of the requirements for those wanting to be on God's side (vv. 14-16). The chapter climaxes in the prophetic promise that God's people will experience the kingdom of God (vv. 17-24).

The woe oracle says it will be done unto you as you have done unto others. The proper response to such a warning is not gleeful celebration that the enemy will get his. Rather the people of God should pray for divine grace and help in light of the international confusion. Everyone hated the ruling nation and its treacherous, destructive practices. Still, the enemy preserved some type of international order. The fall of the great world power could bring even worse chaos.

Despite those conditions, the people expressed their confidence in God, as is often done in the prayers of lament (vv. 5-6). God is "supreme" (v. 5, NEB). His people need fear no international power vacuum. God was finally showing the world who really controls history. Even this did not mean automatic salvation for the people of Judah. God's action had a purpose. He sought to bring justice and righteousness to Jerusalem (see 32:16). This is the foundation for true national and international security. Such salvation is not measured in terms of material prosperity alone (compare 32:15). The abundance of salvation is measured in terms of wisdom and knowledge, terms which can be defined only in light of the Book of Proverbs. Verse 6 summarizes the definition: "the fear of the Lord is his treasure." Other international powers have been despots seeking treasures at the expense of their conquered people. Yahweh was a new kind of international ruler. The only treasure he sought was the respect and trust of his people.

Such confidence sent the people of God into still further lamentation. The situation was just not like that. The translation and meaning of verse 7 is uncertain (see RSV note). Apparently the verse describes the political insecurity of the times, while verse 8 pictures the economic problems. Political envoys were unsuccessful; trade routes could not be traveled; and economic agreements meant nothing. The Hebrew word for "covenant" is singular here, not plural (as in RSV) and may be used in a double sense to refer both to the economic agreements among nations or individuals and to the covenant of Israel with God. Such turmoil in every sphere of life resulted in judgment even on the natural order, where fertility would fade.

God would not ignore the lament of his people. He promised to act (vv. 10-13). But against whom? The call went out to those far off as well as those near to confess the greatness of God or else! (v. 13).

God's people would get the message! Panic associated with the enemies of God in holy war would grip even the inhabitants of Zion. Even they would join the classification—sinners, godless. The latter means they are hypocrites who appear pious to the outward world but actually ignore God in their daily lives. The prophet showed such people the only way to act in the moment of God's judgment, if they desired to make their home as sojourners protected by God from the coming judgment. The references to fire and burning (v. 14) involve a wordplay on fire's role in the Temple sacrifices and its role as instrument in God's judgment on the world.

People who expected to dwell under God's protection must remember what God required of anyone who would enter his Temple to worship. The godly person does not participate in activities which result in cheating the poor, avoiding the proper processes of the court, injuring innocent people, or becoming involved in any type of evil plots or activities (v. 15). To a godly person, God promised true security (v. 16).

For those who have responded properly in the moment of crisis, the prophet offered a promise (v. 17). They would see the Divine

King in all his royal splendor. He would rule a land stretching far beyond the narrow confines of Israel under the Assyrian and Babylonian empires. The terror of foreign oppression and paying out of tribute to foreign rulers, who carefully controlled the military defenses of Israel, would recede into the past, entering the mind only in moments of historical reflection. Then the worshipers could again joyously enter Jerusalem for the annual worship festivals. Never again would Israel have to worship in a movable sanctuary which might be destroyed or carried away by enemies. God would be personally present ruling over his people, who would need no longer to fear the whims and fancies of earthly kings who refused to accept the kingly role defined by God and his prophets (see chs. 1; 11). Sickness would vanish (v. 24) and no longer be understood as the result of sin, because God would forgive the sin of the people. This would be the return to paradise.

We must note that the application of shipping imagery in verses 21 and 23 to Jerusalem is hard to understand. Apparently, the prophet is saying that God will give his people as great a reputation in all areas of life as the two superpowers—Egypt on the Nile and Babylon on the Euphrates. Jerusalem, however, would have no need for the rivers in matters of war or commerce, since God would provide all her needs.

Call to Condemnation (34:1-17)

Oracle against foreign nation. Israel pictured Edom as her closest relation among the nations. Edom came from Israel's brother Esau (Gen. 25:30). Edom received special privileges from Israel's God (Deut. 2:4-5). Edom, identified with the hill country of Seir (Gen. 36:8-9), was Yahweh's mountain residence from which he came to help Israel (Judg. 5:4). Yet Israel continually battled Edom, from the wilderness wanderings onward. Judah's anger against Edom reached its height when Edom joined Babylon in the conquest of Jerusalem (see Obad. 11; Ps. 137:7). Edom became the chief target of Judah's prophetic oracles against her enemies, becoming almost the symbol of anger and hatred.

Isaiah 34 joins the chorus of condemnation by calling the nations of the world, the earth, and the universe as witnesses to the Lord's oath against Edom (v. 1). God's anger was not limited to Edom, however. It reached to "all the nations" (v. 2). Edom's punishment would come as part of a universal judgment by God upon his enemies, a punishment which would not even allow honorable burial.

The text of the chapter is filled with words which are very rare in the Hebrew Bible and thus often defy precise definition. This has caused translators and commentators problems since the earliest translations, so that anyone studying chapter 34 should consult several translations. The chapter pictures in gruesome detail the extent of God's wrath and judgment against his enemies. It is based on a theology of history stated in verse 8. God's control of history may not always be visible. His enemies may appear to have the upper hand. But God is on schedule. He will intervene to bring his opponents to justice. In this case, justice is so complete that the land is left to the wild beasts, creatures of the night (vv. 11-15). (For various understandings of the exact nature of these creatures, compare KJV, RSV, NIV, NEB.)

The authority for such prophecy is that it is a part of the Bible. It is to be found in the "book of the Lord" (v. 16). The prophet claimed authority for his own word and reminded readers that when the fulfillment came, they could come back to the book and check it out. God would do precisely what the prophet said. Here is another indication of the spoken prophetic word becoming written Scripture (see 8:16; 30:8).

The certainty of the prophecy is underlined again (v. 17) by taking up the legal process of dividing property by means of sacred lot (see Josh. 14:2; 18:6). This time, however, the territory of Edom would be allotted to wild beasts rather than to people.

The Return of the Redeemed (35:1-10)

Prophecy of salvation. This section gives the final prophetic sermon prior to the narratives of chapters 36—39. The sermon serves to prepare for the prophetic message of chapters 40—55, bridging the gap between the dark days of Judah's vassalage to Assyria and Babylon and the hope for a new day after the return from captivity. The chapter shines even brighter against the dark background of chapter 34. It forms the climax of the hope for Judah given in chapters 1—39, and, in a way, summarizes the message of the book as a whole.

Israel's hope includes the natural order as well as the human, so that even the most barren desert will bring forth lovely flowers in the day of salvation (contrast 33:9). The only comparison for the newly-budding wilderness would be the fertile plain of Sharon and the fruitful apex of Mount Carmel. The land can have its glory because God reveals his (contrast Ex. 33:18-23).

The revelation of God's majesty provided the background for a new prophetic commission (vv. 3-4). If God could change the dry wasteland so radically, how much more he could do for humanity! The prophet was called then to encourage the weak and feeble. Their reason for fear would vanish. God would come in vengeance. The divine appearance would destroy the enemy (34:8) but bring salvation to the people of God. Such salvation is not limited to a spiritual realm. The sick and disabled would find all their reasons for having an inferiority complex destroyed.

The best was yet to come. God's people would no longer face isolation in a foreign land. God's purified people would pass over to Zion (v. 8). God would provide total safety for the joyous journey. Only the persons God had redeemed from captivity would be allowed on the road. Life would become a festival of singing to Yahweh (v. 10).

Still, we must face the fact that half of human life would be removed in the day of redemption. "Sorrow and sighing shall flee away" (v. 10).

Proof of Prophetic Power (36:1 to 39:8)

701 BC, Prophetic narrative. The last four chapters of the first division of Isaiah's book repeat almost word for word the report of 2 Kings 18:13 to 20:19. A similar report appears in 2 Chronicles 32:1-31. Interestingly enough, we also have an Assyrian record of the events in the Annals of Sennacherib (translated in James B. Pritchard, ed., *Ancient Near Eastern Texts Relating to the Old Testament,* 2nd ed.; Princeton, New Jersey: Princeton University Press, 1955, pp. 287-288).

The very fact that we have four accounts of the events, three of them in the Bible, and each different in its own way, should teach us something about the way we study the Bible. The very fact that God led in the preservation of the three biblical accounts should underline the importance of these narratives. They deserve our close attention.

The distinctiveness of the various accounts reminds us that each serves its own function and purpose within the Bible, so that we must examine the materials closely to determine what each of the narratives is trying to say in its own literary context. One helpful way of doing this is to look precisely at those points where the materials diverge from one another. Often, it is here that the perspective and purpose of the narrative can be found, for it is here that the author is underlining his own point of emphasis. Our task is to see what the narrative says in the context of the Book of Isaiah.

We learn from Sennacherib's report that he forced the king of Sidon to escape to Cyprus and set up a new "puppet king." He received tribute from kings of Byblos, Ashdod, Beth-Ammon, Moab, and Edom. He exiled the king of Ashkelon to Assyria, replacing him with a former king who paid him tribute. Ekron rebelled against their king, handing him over to Hezekiah and trusting Egypt to help them. Sennacherib faced the Ethiopian king of Egypt as Eltekeh and won, then restored the king of Ekron. He conquered forty-six cities of Judah and countless small villages, capturing over two hundred thousand people. He made Hezekiah "like a bird in a cage" in Jerusalem and then forced him to send heavy tribute to Nineveh, Hezekiah's army having deserted him.

The biblical account shows that Hezekiah surrendered to Sennacherib, paying heavy tribute (2 Kings 18:14-16), but it is more interested in other developments. The account in Isaiah contains only these other matters. This shows us its center of interest. It seeks to illustrate the authority and power of God and his prophet in the midst of extreme political crisis.

Assyria Asserts Authority (36:1-22)

The central theme of the narrative complex is that of authority. Thus the opening episode shows the Assyrian claim to total power in face of king Hezekiah and his God, Yahweh. The dating "In the fourteenth year" (v. 1) of Hezekiah would mean that Hezekiah began to reign in 715 BC. This stands in some tension to the note in 1 Kings 18:1 that he began to reign in the third year of Hoshea of Israel, which would be 729 or 728 BC. It may be that Hezekiah was named crown prince or began to share royal duties with his father at the earlier date.

Rabshakeh (v. 2) apparently means "chief cup-bearer." The exact duties are not known to us, but he was certainly one of the highest ranking diplomats in the Assyrian court. Lachish would have been one of the first stops on Sennacherib's tour of destruction in Judah. This shows us that verse one represents a summary of all that Sennacherib did rather than the chronological starting point from which the remainder of the narrative follows. The Assyrian official was a diplomat, not a military officer. The accompanying military force was to protect him, not to begin the battle against Jerusalem. The meeting place was where Isaiah confronted Ahaz earlier (7:3). Hezekiah sent his chief officials (see ch. 22).

The central word of the narrative is *trust,* the Hebrew word appearing in various forms eight times in 36:4-7,9; 37:10. Rabshakeh listed the various possibilities: 1. Trust wise battle strategy despite lack of a powerful army (v. 5); 2. Trust Egypt, despite the repeated proof that Pharaoh bites the hand that feeds him (v. 6); 3. Trust Yahweh, your God, despite the fact that Hezekiah had destroyed all his altars (2 Kings 18:4)—an argument which would appeal to the people who loved to use the ancient worship places outside Jerusalem, even when God's messengers condemned such practices (v. 7).

In face of such a situation, the Assyrian was willing to supply weapons for Judah, because she did not even have the soldiers to use them (vv. 8-9). Sennacherib did not fear Yahweh, because he possessed a copy of a treaty with Hezekiah sworn under oath in the name of the God of Israel as well as of the gods of Assyria. Hezekiah had broken the treaty, so that Assyria could claim that she marched against Jerusalem in the name of the God of the treaty (v. 10).

Assyria was not the only one with protective soldiers. Judah's soldiers sat on the city wall protecting their envoys. The envoys were in such a delicate situation they did not want even the loyal soldiers to understand the bargaining process, so they pled for use of the official diplomatic language rather than the local vernacular (v. 11). This encouraged Rabshakeh to shout louder, explicitly including the soldiers in the conversations. The soldiers faced a choice—trust King Hezekiah and his theological promises (v. 15) or trust the king of Assyria to provide food rather than starvation in the present moment and a permanent home just like this one in the exotic and powerful land of Assyria for the future (vv. 16-17). History proved theological promises empty, claimed Rabshakeh. Even Samaria, also a city of Yahweh, fell (v. 19).

Hezekiah's messengers had been commissioned to listen, not talk, so they returned to their master, but in a state of mourning (v. 22). Assyrian authority had been asserted, Hezekiah's and Yahweh's denied. The tussle of trust was on.

A Ruler's Righteousness Rewarded (37:1-38)

The king joined the mourning rites, but did so in the proper manner and place. He went to God's house with his complaints and sent to God's prophet for advice (contrast ch. 7). Hezekiah wanted God to take vengeance on those who would dare to mock the true God (v. 4). Isaiah replied with an oracle of salvation (v. 6).

The triumphal procession of Sennacherib drew nearer (v. 8), but the Egyptian Pharaoh was not as undependable as the Assyrians thought. He came to help (v. 9). Sennacherib tried to hurry up the bargaining process (v. 10). The Assyrian king took up another argument often used by his enemies: Yahweh would protect his capital city where his holy dwelling stood. The Assyrian king claimed that the evidence of history has proved this wrong (vv. 12-13).

Hezekiah again displayed his trust in Yahweh (v. 14). This trust was based on the theological confession of Yahweh as the universal Creator who continues to control creation (v. 16). Hezekiah took seriously the Assyrian arguments, but drew a sharp distinction between the gods that were the creations of human hands defeated by Assyria in the past and the Creator who held the world in his hands and now confronted the Assyrians (v. 19).

On such a theological basis, Hezekiah cried to Yahweh to prove himself among the nations. Victory itself had a theological purpose, not just a selfish reason for the king alone (v. 20).

God again used the prophet to communicate his response (v. 21). Sennacherib was pictured as a lover trying to court the young virgin Jerusalem, but the girl showed her spirit by refusing all advances (v. 22). God rose to protect his daughter and rebuke the insolence of Sennacherib. God, not Sennacherib, was in charge of human history and had planned the course of events (v. 26). Sennacherib had no future in Judah. God told him to go back where he came from (v. 29).

Isaiah had a message not only for Sennacherib. He also had a word for Hezekiah. The Assyrian siege had destroyed the crops. God would provide enough food through what came up wild for two years. Then the normal agricultural activities could resume (v. 30). This would be a symbol of Judah's growth, which appeared as dead as the farm crops (vv. 31-32). Isaiah's message is summarized in verses 33-35. Jerusalem would not see fighting. God would defend his city to protect his own reputation and to protect the promises he had made to David (see 2 Sam. 7).

God proved as good as his word (vv. 36-37). The death of Sennacherib did occur in political revolt (v. 38) in the year 681 BC. Assyrian annals report that he was smashed over the head with the images of protective deities. The divine name Nisroch is not known in any other ancient document. Ararat is known as Urartu in Assyrian records and centered in Lake Van in Armenia.

Prayer, the Proper Prescription (38:1-22)

The narrative shifts its center of interest from national welfare to the personal health of the king. As a by-product, it shows us how ancient Israel understood one part of the prophetic office and how it understood the prayer relationship between people and God.

Here is the first time in the narrative (chs. 36—39) that Isaiah faced Hezekiah personally. The prophet had a stern prognosis: death. Hezekiah, however, found the proper prescription: prayer. The content of the prayer is interesting. As so often in the Psalms (see Pss. 7; 17; 26; 59), a confession of innocence appears. The Israelite did not take his struggles sitting down. He was not ready immediately to accept the total blame for the situation. When he did not think he deserved the fate he received, he went straight to God with his complaint. Hezekiah's was not a self-righteous attitude. It was a bitter wrestling to understand the personal relationship with God. For Hezekiah, it involved bitter tears (v. 3).

God listened to such a sincere cry and sent his prophet back with a new word (vv. 4-8). Here we must note the understanding of prophecy this involves. The prophet had to contradict his earlier message (v. 1). God remained free to respond to prayer even when it involved changing what he had previously proclaimed. Personal relationship with his people, not a predetermined divine plan, predominated for God. The prophet understood this and was willing to be God's instrument, even if his own reputation might be called in question as one who said first one thing, then another.

The prophetic promise answered not only the personal problem of the king, but it also extended the hope to the nation (v. 6). God underscored his determination to answer prayer by giving a spectacular sign to Hezekiah (vv. 7-8). The exact nature of the sign is hard to understand because the Hebrew text is not clear at this point (compare several translations). Rather than a sundial as interpreted by RSV (v. 8), a staircase of some type is probably meant. The date of the event is also uncertain, since the narrative is in theological order, as with the entire Book of Isaiah, rather than in chronological order.

Hezekiah prayed not only in time of trouble. He returned to God with a prayer of thanksgiving formed like many in the Psalms (for example, Pss. 9; 18; 34; 116; 118). Hezekiah revealed his inner emotions in the time of trouble (vv. 10-12) and related how he turned to God (vv. 13-16), concluding with his response of praise and thanksgiving to the mighty miracle (vv. 17-20).

The prayer reveals clearly the Hebrew understanding of death which was that the dead live in Sheol (see 5:14). They were separated from God and humanity, without home or work, and could no longer sing praise to God. They had no more hope (see v. 18). Such an understanding shows how good the gospel news of resurrection really is. The poem separates the final two verses from the position they occupied in 2 Kings 20:7-8, the Isaiah text underlining Hezekiah's righteousness by concluding with his desire to go to the house of worship.

Frightful Future Foreshadowed (39:1-8)

The final narrative points back to the beginning of the oracles against the nations (ch. 13) and points forward to the announcement of deliverance from Babylonian captivity in chapters 40—55. Merodach-baladan was a Babylonian prince who rebelled against Assyria and gained independence lasting from 721 until 710 BC, when Sargon defeated him and took over the Babylonian throne for himself. Merodach-baladan was exiled but continued to stir up trouble, regaining his independence briefly in 703 BC. In this latter period he sent his messengers to Jerusalem to encourage revolt in the west, so that Assyria would have to fight on two fronts. Hezekiah showed the messengers all his resources which could be used in the revolt. Isaiah was furious. He had attempted all along to persuade the Judean kings that they had to lean on God, not on foreign alliances, for help against Assyria.

The prophet had ominous news. Babylon was the next major enemy for Judah. Babylon, not Assyria, would carry away all Judah's treasures. This refers to the first major defeat of Jerusalem in 597 BC (see 2 Kings 24:10-17). Our narrative says that defeat had its origins in a king who became proud and selfish, ignoring the prophetic warning, and accepting prophetic judgment as long as it did not affect him personally (v. 8). A righteous king could save Jerusalem (chs. 37—38), but a selfish king paved the way for its downfall (ch. 39). On this note, the first section of the Book of Isaiah ends, preparing for the second, a word of hope in the hour of horror.

Prospects After Punishment
40:1 to 55:13

The historical focus changes dramatically with chapter 40. We begin to breathe the air of 545 BC. Cyrus of Persia occupied center stage politically (41:2; 44:28; 45:1,13; 46:11; 48:14-15). Israel was living in Babylon, not Jerusalem (42:24; 43:14; 47:1; 48:14). The prophet's declarations of disaster disappear. Only hope from heaven appears. The whole section is a call of comfort to the captives, joined with arguments trying to convince them to accept the comfort God has offered.

The Call to Comfort (40:1-11)

Military chain of command. Isaiah's call to condemnation appeared in chapter 6. Chapter 40 contrasts to this a call to comfort. This call appears like a military order passed through the troops, occurring in four stages:

1. The command apparently began in the heavenly council (see ch. 6) with a call to its members to go to the aid of "my people." As in chapter 6, so here, the prophet was present in the council.

2. The prophet reported to the people in verse 3 relaying the call to action from "our God."

3. The prophet continued to report in verse 6, but then realized

that the new command was no longer in the plural to the people but in the singular, addressing him personally. He reacted with a question, expressing his inability to fulfill the assignment, as occurred so frequently in the prophetic experiences (see 6:5). His complaint received a blunt answer (v. 8).

4. The prophet relayed the message to Jerusalem, that is, to the people of Judah now in exile in Babylon but claiming Jerusalem as their hometown. Jerusalem was called to its own mission. It was to become an army messenger bringing the news of victory back to the cities of Judah (v. 9).

Each element of the chain of command deserves careful consideration, since it opens in summary form an important section of the Bible. The prophetic task has changed from hardening God's people (ch. 6) to comforting them. Such comfort was God's reaction to the lamentations of his people, who had cried that they had no comforter (Lam. 1:2,9,16-17,12; 2:13). Human strength could provide no comfort. The people were reminded that "your God," that is not Babylon's god, but Yahweh, the God of Israel, could provide comfort.

The content of such comfort became clear quickly. Her "time of service" (RSV note), "hard service" (NIV), "term of bondage" (NEB) had ended. The captivity in Babylon was interpreted as work which a prisoner of war had to do for his captor. God announced unexpectedly that the prisoner had been pardoned. This was done both in secular and religious categories. Outwardly, Judah appeared to be a captive of Babylon because she was militarily the weaker party. Seen from a higher perspective, she was Yahweh's prisoner because she had sinned against him.

Yahweh was ready to release Judah. Babylon was not. Yahweh proclaimed that Judah had taken double punishment from the hand of Yahweh. This was in line with the Israelite law which required reimbursement plus payment for damages in certain crimes (Ex. 22:1,7,9).

As Israel first experienced salvation by escape into the wilderness, God planned a new wilderness experience. To prepare for this, he called for a highway to be built. This imitated Babylonian practices in which a highway was built for the great religious festivals so that the images of the gods could be paraded before the people. Yahweh's highway was not to show off his beautiful artwork and clothing. It was to deliver his people in a moment of historical crisis.

Such a highway was to be flat so that God's people would have no trouble crossing it as they followed their God to freedom. This historical act would reveal the true glory of God to the entire world, for God would accomplish what Babylon was not ready to do. God would show his historical power over the majestic kingdom of Babylon. Such news seemed unbelievable to a people so far from home. The prophet said it was sure, because its source was God himself.

Even with such assurance, the prophet was taken by surprise when God called him to preach (v. 6). He sounded the common complaint of his people. Humanity had lost its meaning, being no more significant than grass, which springs up only to be mowed down (v. 6). The sense of the Hebrew of verse 6 is not conveyed by "beauty" (RSV) or "glory" (NIV) or "goodliness" (KJV), but no other English word is better. The original expression is often used for the grace or steadfast love of God to human beings (for example Ex. 34:6; 20:6) and of the devotion people should show to God and to one another (Hos. 2:19; 4:1; 6:4). In this text, the term apparently indicates all the grace and graces of humanity. It is that for which people may be trusted and relied upon. God's breath (which could also be translated wind or spirit) had destroyed all which humanity had to offer. So, the prophet complained, Why preach to people whose reactions are meaningless anyway?

God answered (v. 8), agreeing that human perspective and potential offered no hope. Comfort comes not from mankind but from God. His word is reliable, and he promised comfort.

The prophet finally fulfilled his mission, calling upon Jerusalem to take up her "high mountain" (watchpost) and relay the news of victory (v. 9). Such news did not depend upon a battle which had been fought. Victory was won because "God comes" (v. 10). The coming of God is the content of comfort!

The Creator Comes to Comfort (40:12-31)

Legal dispute. The prophet took his audience to court and brought forth legal arguments to prove the incomparable nature of the God of Israel over against the claims of all other "gods," especially those of Babylon. Only the Creator knows the earth's measurements (v. 12). His Spirit, not the counselors of the Babylonian king, has all wisdom and knowledge (vv. 13-14). In his measuring scales, the heavies among the nations weigh no more than the dust which naturally collects on scales (vv. 14-17). The other gods are only creations of human hands; they did not create the universe (vv. 18-20).

Earthly rulers and kings are grasshoppers when viewed from God's heavenly throne. They are weak plants which God's storm wind blows away (vv. 21-24). God is so powerful that he created the hosts of heaven and so intelligent that he knows each by name (vv. 25-26). In face of the greatness and wisdom of God, the prophet addressed Judah with a series of questions (vv. 27-28) showing them the weakness of their faith and the ridiculous nature of their complaints, complaints which he himself had shared (v. 6).

The Creator who knew the names of all the stars certainly knew the problems of his own chosen people (v. 27). He would certainly give strength to his people even in a time so trying that the youngest and strongest warriors were totally exhausted. This was the comfort which the Creator conceived for his confused and concerned creatures. The way was opening for Israel to run home to her fatherland and to her Father.

Conquerors Called to Court (41:1-7)

Concluding legal summary. The prophet pictured God addressing the international courtroom and summarizing his case against the foreign "gods." Afterwards, the nations would have a chance to summarize their case (v. 1). God's courtroom argument was quite simple. He pointed to history and asked, Who is responsible for the unexpected victories of Cyrus? (vv. 2-3). The description probably points to Cyrus's victories over the Medes and Lydians. To answer the question of verses 2-3, God raised another question (v. 4a): Who has always done this? Who has directed history from the beginning? The answer is blunt—Yahweh, who was the first Being and who will be with the last being. The God of Israel had proved through his surprising historical actions that he and he only is God.

The "peoples" called to prepare their case in verse 1 could not respond. They simply trembled in fear and tried to encourage their neighbor (vv. 5-7). They had come and drawn near as told to do in verse 1, but that was all they could do. With ironic genius, the prophet pictured the reaction of the craftsmen who made the idols. They told each other how good their work was (v. 7). But this was only a last hurrah. They had lost both their religion and their business. This, too, was comfort for God's people.

The Savior Soothes His Servant (41:8-20)

Oracle of salvation. The prophet moved from the courtroom to the Temple to announce salvation for his people. He began by using Abraham to remind God's people of all that God had done for them, a surprisingly rare reference to the patriarch in prophecy. The purpose was to show Israel that she was defined by God's acts and purposes not by her own power and accomplishments.

Israel was the servant of God. This expression includes two meanings. First, Israel was the political vassal who served King Yahweh and was dependent upon him for all her political power. Second, Israel in her laments to Yahweh had confessed his authority by referring to itself as servants. In Isaiah 40—66 "servant" became a major theological theme.

Israel was servant of God because she had been chosen by God. God sought in love one people from all the nations to worship him and him alone. The destruction in 587 BC did not annul God's election, but rather confirmed that election included responsibility and mission.

God's choice involved seeking Abraham in the eastern end of the earth and then bringing Israel up from Egypt in the western end. Finally, God returned to Babylon and to Egypt to bring the exiles back to the place he had chosen for them. The word of election was thus a word of comfort and not a reason for fear.

God's choice of Israel resulted not only in help and victory for Israel (v. 10) but destruction and shame for her enemies (vv. 11-12). God's help would enable Israel to overcome all obstacles in her path back to her land (vv. 15-16; see 40:3-4). The purpose was that Israel might quit complaining and lamenting and return to rejoicing in the great acts which God accomplished for her. God would not only prepare the way and get rid of all obstacles, but also he would provide all the needs on the way (vv. 17-19). Again, God had a purpose in this. He wanted people to know that he was still active in history. The defeat of Jerusalem was not the end of the line for the Holy One of Israel.

Indictment Against the Idols (41:21-29)

Courtroom trial. God called the gods of Babylon to court (see 40:12-31). One issue was decisive. Who could predict history and carry out the predictions? (v. 22). The gods could not meet the test. They could do nothing at all, neither good nor bad, and so were proved to be nothing (vv. 23-24).

Over against this stood the testimony of Yahweh. He had called Cyrus to take over world rule (v. 25). The Hebrew text of verses 25-27 has not been well preserved, so that the precise meaning and translation is often difficult. The Dead Sea Scrolls in verse 25 read, "He called by his name," which may mean that God called Cyrus by name (see 45:1). In verse 26 God continued to question the gods without success. Yahweh had spoken the first word to Jerusalem through his herald (compare 40:9). No other god had said a word.

The court decision was clear. Only Yahweh stood the test. The "gods" were created images, just a bunch of hot air (v. 29). Yahweh alone directed and interpreted world history.

Servant Sent in the Spirit (42:1-4)

Formal introduction. This is the first of four Servant Songs in Isaiah 40—55 (see also 49:1-6; 50:4-9; 52:13 to 53:12). Here God formally presented the servant to an audience, though both the name of the servant and the nature of the audience remain mysteriously unclear. Apparently God installed the servant in an important official office (see 2 Kings 22:12).

The servant gained power for his mission from the divine Spirit just as had earlier rulers and prophets. The servant's task was to "bring forth justice to the nations" (v. 1). "Justice" involves a much broader meaning than the English term. In verse 4 it stands parallel to Torah, law or teaching. It is the verdict handed down by a judge (2 Kings 25:6); the whole court process (Isa. 3:14); the gracious and merciful judgment of God (Isa. 30:18); or the natural right and order claimed by a person or group of persons (Ex. 23:6; Isa. 10:2; 40:27). In our text, the term apparently encompasses a broad meaning of the natural world order and right expected by the nations of the earth now restored by the gracious and merciful judgment of God on the basis of his law or teaching.

The way the servant was to accomplish his task is surprising. He would not be a street preacher or political rebel seeking to arouse the population, nor a royal messenger reading the king's proclamations (v. 2). The servant had been given royal power by the Divine King, but he would exercise that power in such a way that he would not even damage that which appears useless and ready to be discarded (v. 3).

The servant would finally succeed. "Faithfully" (v. 3) should be translated "he will bring to reality" with an undertone of lasting, enduring, implied. Justice would prevail! The servant would not suffer the fate of the useless utensils of verse 3 until he could report to his King, "Mission accomplished" (compare 2:3). Matthew saw in the healing ministry of Jesus the fulfillment of the first Servant Song (Matt. 12:17-21).

A Covenant for the Countries (42:5-9)

Oracle of installation. Having introduced the servant to the audience, God spoke directly to the servant through a prophetic oracle. He began by quoting a familiar hymn (v. 5) praising him as Creator. This confirmed his power and importance for all people who walk and breathe. God then confirmed his servant in the high office (v. 6). This was done in "righteousness." Such a statement does not repeat the obvious, that God is righteous. Rather, it defines the power given the new official. God gave him the power to restore the right in the world, that is to bring salvation. The translation and meaning of "kept you" remains uncertain. It may mean "I have formed you" (NEB). God's purpose for the newly-installed servant was clear. He represented God's covenant, God's promise to the nations to bring light into their darkness. This was explicitly described (v. 7) as help for the helpless.

The tone switches suddenly in verse 8. God reminded the newly-installed servant of his limits. Yahweh alone must receive proper honor and praise. Worship of other gods or their images was forbidden. Why? Because (v. 9) God had proven himself to be God in his acts in history and would do so again through the servant. The "you" of verse 9 is plural, not singular, so that God's announcement and warning (v. 8) is applied not just to the servant but to a larger audience, the people of God who have sung the hymn of verse 5 in their worship for lo these many years.

The major question remains unanswered. Who was this servant commissioned by Yahweh? At one time, it may have had a definite historical reference. Commentators have often thought of Cyrus (see 44:28; 45:1). But within the written Scripture it became a promise of God's future actions through a people or an individual who would accept the commission of God. Jesus of Nazareth is the God-man who has taken such a commission seriously and brought it into reality.

Thanksgiving for Triumph (42:10-13)

Hymn. This passage functions almost as the closing hymn for the preceding installation. It is a call to the world to celebrate God's new action. It resembles Psalms 96, 98, 149. For "Kedar" (v. 11), see Isaiah 21:16-17. For "Sela," which may simply mean rock, see 16:1. The new act is seen as holy war led by Yahweh (see Ex. 15:3). The enemy will fall. Let all the world rejoice.

The Moment to March (42:14-17)

Promise of salvation. Israel, exiled in Babylon, tended to think God had lost his power or had totally forgotten his people. The prophet rose to say that God knew that he had not acted for them in a long time. Now God had had enough. He could stand the pain of separation from his people no longer. He would cry out like a woman giving birth and spring into action for his people. He would destroy all natural obstacles and prepare a path through the wilderness back home for his blind people. Deliverance of God's people had a theological consequence. People who had given up on God and given glory to graven gods must face the consequences (v. 17).

Salvation for the Sightless Servant (42:18 to 43:13)

Oracle of salvation following a dispute. The prophet of salvation met as much opposition as did those who prophesied doom. Here we see clearly the hot debate that ensued between prophet and unbelieving audience. Finally, the prophet resorted to name calling to get the audience's attention. The people of God saw themselves as the servant of God, but they did not see their role the same as did the prophet (compare 42:1-9). So the prophet declared they were blind and deaf!

Israel did not understand what God was doing in their history (v 20). God had chosen to glorify his Torah, his instruction for his people because God was righteous and wanted to restore the right (see 42:6). The people had not listened to God's instructions. Blind and deaf, they had marched into exile and found themselves imprisoned, at the mercy of their captors, with no one powerful enough to rescue them (v. 22). Apparently the people used this situation to mock the prophet and claim their hopelessness. The prophet took up their mocking words and threw them back in their faces, concluding with the bitter question of verse 23.

Would anyone really assume the role of the servant of Yahweh as pictured by the prophet? Or would they remain blind? They had every reason to answer the prophetic call. After all, the present situation was caused by God (vv. 24-25). He could act again and was at that moment calling his people to accept the new role he had for them.

The basis of such a call was the oracle of salvation (43:1-7), which promised God's people that even in exile they had no reason for fear. The God who had created Israel was now redeeming her from captivity. He would overcome all obstacles (43:2; compare 42:15). They could count on the Lord, the Holy One of Israel, their Savior. Once God had delivered Israel from Egypt. Now he was ready to give Egypt to the new world ruler, to Cyrus of Persia, in exchange for the freedom of his people. What a huge ransom for such a little nation! How God did love his people! God was ready to do whatever was necessary to bring all his people from their places of exile around the globe (vv. 5-6). He had created them for his glory (v. 7; compare v. 1) and now would restore them for his glory.

Having given the promise of salvation, the prophet returned to his dispute with his audience, taking up again the language of the courtroom. He resumed his name calling (see 42:18) as he assembled the people of God as both jury and witnesses at the same time. Then he called the other nations to join the process. He directed the first question to the nations (v. 9). Could they defend the rights of their gods? Turning to his own people, he swore them in as his witnesses (v. 10) and proclaimed that they were his servants, thus reinstalling them in the office which they had refused to use properly (see 42:19).

As servants of Yahweh, the people of God had one mission. They must understand and trust in the nature of their God as the Creator, the Savior, the only God. They must be totally loyal to him and to no other (vv. 10-12). They themselves could look at their own past history which proved the validity of the claim God made for himself (v. 12). From the Exodus onward, God had delivered Israel and proclaimed his word to her. Now was the time for the blind servants to open their eyes to God's actions and for the deaf servants to open their ears to his words. Then they could open their mouths as witnesses to the claim of Yahweh to have a monopoly on deity.

We must note that the translation and interpretation of verse 12 is difficult. "When there was no strange god among you" reads literally, "and not among you all a strange one." It can be present or past tense. The strange one may mean (1) strange god; (2) that Yahweh was not a stranger; (3) there were no foreigners; or (4) that there were no outsiders among them who had not heard the news. This last sense may well be correct, the prophet qualifying his audience as witnesses by saying that they knew all that God had said and done and could testify to it.

The conclusion is that God will continue to be what he has always been, the God and Savior of Israel. The message of deliverance from Babylonian captivity was not crazy. It simply fitted the pattern of how God had always acted with his people. No one had power to stop God from acting as he chose (v. 13). Would Israel wake up, believe, and witness to this God?

Breaking the Bars of Babylon (43:14-21)

Promise of salvation. The prophet had one concrete word of promise to give to the exiles in Babylon. God would defeat Babylon! The basis of such a promise lay in the nature of God, the Holy One who could endure no imperfection in himself; the Creator of Israel, who would not permit his people to perish; the King of Israel, who ruled their destiny. Notice that the second half of verse 14 is so obscure (RSV note) that translation is impossible. The Hebrew text says, "And Chaldeans in ships their shouts." Even the term "bars" is uncertain, sometimes being interpreted as "fugitives" (NIV) or "nobles" (KJV).

On the basis of God's new word and his consistent character, the prophet drew the consequences (vv. 16-21). The God of the Exodus (vv. 16-17) had something new for them. They must forget the past and its problems, give up the idea that Yahweh was only the god of the good old days, and look forward to God's new act. Be ready to be surprised by God! God had a new exodus through a new wilderness ready for his people (vv. 19-20) so that the people might sing a new hymn to God (v. 21).

The Spirit to Save Sinful Servants (43:22 to 44:5)

Oracle of salvation following a legal appeal. The problems of the prophet with his audience appear again. He had to answer accusations which they made against Yahweh. He began with a counter accusation. Israel forgot God (vv. 22-23a). They were tired of him and did not wear themselves out to serve him. For burnt offerings, see Leviticus 1; for sacrifices, Leviticus 3. The prophet spoke to Israel about how she had acted through his history. Certainly, when she had a Temple, Israel loved to bring sacrifices (see Isa. 1:11). Such sacrifices did not express devotion nor bring honor to Yahweh.

Indeed, the situation was quite different. God, the Divine King, had not caused Israel to serve like a vassal king or slave by demanding hard-to-prepare cereal offerings (23b; compare Leviticus 2) nor had he worn them out with expensive and hard-to-get frankincense, which might be seen as tribute brought to a king. The other side of the picture was (v. 24) that Israel had not gone the extra mile and paid out her hard-earned money for a special present for Yahweh nor had she been able with her sacrifices to meet a physical need for Yahweh. The case was that Israel had tried to turn Yahweh into a servant rather than a master (24b), so that Yahweh became weary from trying to deal with Israel. Israel, not Yahweh, was guilty and deserved to be brought to court.

Israel had to be reminded again who her God really was. He was not an unreasonable taskmaster nor a weakling, panting longingly until Israel came to put a pittance at his door. Yahweh, the God of Israel, was the one who had repeatedly forgiven and forgotten Israel's sin in order to accomplish his own purposes (v. 25). This he was doing again. Certainly, God was not guilty.

Now, God issued the challenge to Israel to come to court and argue the case with him (v. 26). He reminded them that since their father Jacob (see v. 22) Israel's history had been a history of sin, exemplified in her "mediators" or more probably "spokesmen" (v. 27, NIV; NEB), that is, in her political leaders. The history of sin led even the forgiving God to remove the holiness of the leaders of worship who had led the people astray in their sacrificial acts and to deliver the nation over to total ruin, so that their enemies could poke fun and mock them (v. 28).

God was not finished with his history of forgiveness. God remained free even when his people tried to enslave him. Despite the events of 586 BC, Israel remained God's servant, his chosen people (44:1). He would revive his dried-up people with the life-giving Spirit and with a renewal of the blessing to Abraham (Gen. 12:2; 13:16). Everyone would be proud to be an Israelite, a worshiper of Yahweh (v. 5). Yes, God's people, not God, were guilty. God was free to punish them, but he also was free to forgive them and promise them a new future. Could the people of God believe such a promise or would they continue to accuse God?

Ours Is the Only One! (44:6-8)

Oracle of salvation. The prophet repeated what became his central message. God has proved that he is the only God (40:12-31; 41:4,21-24,29; 42:8,17; 43:10-13). No one else had dared to reveal his historical plans to his people as had Yahweh. Israel had no reason to fear. She could trust Yahweh to keep his word even in the lowest point of her history, the Babylonian Exile. They were witnesses to the history of prophecy, the history of God proving his claim to be the only God, the only refuge, the only one worthy of trust.

Idolators Are Idiots (44:9-20)

Song of mocking. Israel despised the mocking she received from
her enemies. She herself became expert in using the same language, as we see clearly here. The prophet described carefully and
sarcastically the process involved in making the gods of the nations.
What resulted was what had existed when God began to create the
earth—nothing, the same word translated "without form" in Genesis 1:2, perhaps better translated simply "chaos." Skilled workers
wore themselves out (v. 12) and ended up with "an abomination, . . .
a block of wood . . . ashes . . . a lie in my right hand" (vv. 19-20).
Such people deserved their fate—being put to shame (v. 11),
producing only the beauty of man rather than the power and glory of
deity (v. 13), being robbed of the remainder of their kindling wood
(v. 15), expecting deliverance out of trouble from something their
own hands had produced (v. 17). They had lost all powers of reason
and were as blind as Israel had been (v. 18; compare 42:18; 43:8).

The sad undertone of the passage is that Israel wanted to accuse
Yahweh (see 43:22) and worship the images created by the Babylonians (see 42:8,17; 43:10-12).

Remember Your Redeemer (44:21-28)

Call to repentance. The prophet reminded his audience once
more of their true identity. They were Israel, the servant of Yahweh,
created by God and never forgotten by him. God had already begun
work to redeem them through the activities of Cyrus of Persia (v. 28).
Israel must do her part in response to God's actions. She must
remember what God had done and was doing and must turn away
from her sins and the gods of Babylon to her Redeemer (vv. 21-22).
She must join in the hymns of praise to her Redeemer (v. 23). "Will
be glorified in Israel" (v. 23) is better translated "displays his glory in
Israel" (NIV).

Yet another task awaited Israel. She had to listen to the royal
proclamation of the Divine King (vv. 24-28), as he announced his
new political platform. God first laid the basis for his program by
explaining precisely who he is: the Creator (v. 24), the source of true
prophecy and the enemy of all Babylon's false prophets and wise

men (vv. 25-26). Then God described his program as he promised to rebuild Jerusalem and Judah for his people (v. 26), to destroy the chaotic world ruler Babylon, so proud of her position on the mighty Euphrates River (v. 27), and to use Cyrus, king of Persia, as his shepherd, a term often used for kings, to fulfill his purpose of rebuilding Jerusalem, with its Temple.

When the exiles in Babylon heard the political program of Yahweh, they had to be shocked that he would use a foreign king rather than someone from the line of David. Dare they believe the prophet, lay aside their fasting and mourning rites along with their Babylonian gods, and take up the mighty hymn offered them by the prophet?

Calling Cyrus to Conquest and Construction (45:1-13)

Installation ceremony. Here is the center of the political message of Isaiah 40—55. The prophet pictured the installation of Cyrus in the office as Yahweh's anointed one, his messiah (v. 1). Yahweh took Cyrus by the hand (see 42:6) and described the mission he had for the newly-installed messiah. He was to defeat the nations, particularly Babylon (vv. 1-2) and receive the treasures in the hidden store places as his deserved tribute (v. 3). God did this to introduce himself to Cyrus and to show Cyrus that he was only a vassal king under the Divine King, the God of Israel.

Yahweh did not act simply for Cyrus' sake (v. 4). He acted for his servant Israel's sake. God could use someone who did not even know about him to do his will in order to help his people. Yahweh could do this because he had no competition. He was the only God (v. 5). He used Cyrus in order to spread the news around the world that only one God ruled the universe (v. 6). God thus stepped outside the confines of Israel to use another world power to accomplish his purposes in order to widen the arena in which his purposes were recognized and honored. This meant, however, that God was responsible for all of world history, creating both the good and the bad (v. 7).

Having installed Cyrus, God was ready to get things moving. He commanded the heavenly powers to join the earthly in bringing forth righteousness, the proper world order, and salvation, the proper status for humanity. This would show that God not only created the darkness of the Exile but could also create the light of a new day of salvation and right (v. 8).

Despite his assurances, God had to argue further with his people and did so by using prophetic woe oracles against those who disagreed with him (vv. 9-10). He first set them in their place as creatures, mere babes powerless to argue against the Creator, the heavenly parent. Then he became specific. Could anyone accuse God of misusing his own children, his own creatures? Could he not treat his children as he desired? Did anyone know a better way than that of their Father? Could anyone claim that God was misusing the world and its inhabitants when he installed Cyrus as his messiah? After all, God is the creator of all people (v. 12).

So God concluded with the simple explanation of what he was doing with the works of his own hands. He had called Cyrus to restore the right order in the universe (see 42:6; 45:8). This centered on the right order for God's people in their own land with their own city (v. 13). God had not hired Cyrus for such work as a king might hire a professional warrior or a vassal king. Rather, God had installed Cyrus in the office of messiah to perform the task God had given him. Cyrus was God's official, not God's hireling (v. 13).

Evangelizing the Enemy (45:14-25)

Courtroom speeches. This is a very complex unit which has been interpreted in many different ways. Yet it is a very important section, containing some of the central theological points of the book. It begins with an announcement of salvation for Israel, which is then defended against arguments which the prophet's opponents brought against him.

The action of Cyrus (45:1-13) would bring Egypt and her African allies to their knees (v. 14; see 43:3-4), but they would not pay tribute to Cyrus. Rather, they would follow a feminine singular "you," which dominates this section. This must be Zion/Jerusalem. Their reason would not be political, but theological. These African nations would recognize in the work of Cyrus the power of Israel's God (see 45:6). This led them to one of the great theological insights of the Bible (v. 15). The God of Israel was not a God of pompous show and procession, tooting his own horn at every corner. He did not always act openly and clearly through the normal means expected in the ancient Near East. Rather, he often acted quietly, where people had to be very perceptive and attentive to see and understand what he was doing. Even his own people remained quite blind to many of his activities (43:8). He did not even have to work with his own people. He could work through a foreign ruler like Cyrus (see also 10:5). Yet when a person finally understood what God was doing, the only reaction was the cry of praise, "O God of Israel, the Savior" (v. 15).

The other side to the proclamation was the recognition of the worthlessness of other claims to the divine throne (v. 16; see 44:9-20) on the one hand, and the significance for God's people on the other hand. God's people would be saved (v. 17), a central biblical theme, and certainly central for the Book of Isaiah. For Israel, salvation was a very concrete term which meant help in time of trouble, particularly deliverance in war from the enemy and deliverance in the courtroom from the accuser. The precise opposite is "to be put to shame" (v. 17), that is, to lose the case or the battle, to let the enemy win. The prophet thus looked to the day when Israel would no longer have to call on God to win her battles or to restore her social order. He would have done it once and for all.

The problem was that the prophet's audience did not believe him. They claimed that God had returned everything to chaos (vv. 18-19). The prophet answered, Oh, no! Look back to the beginning. God did not create chaos. He changed chaos into a world where people could live. Chaos is the world of the Babylonian gods whose diviners and prophets have to go into darkness, even into the world of the dead, to find the word of their god. But our God gave his word through his prophet out in the open just like he always has (v. 19). Won't you believe the promise of God even though it involves the hiddenness of using Cyrus rather than coming himself in a mighty miracle? God's word brings truth or right (the same word as in 42:6). He speaks straight. What more can you want?

The dispute was not only with God's people, who would not believe God's new word of promise. God also sought to work with the nations. Therefore, he called them to court (v. 20). He charged them with serving worthless gods who could not save. Again God's evidence was simple, predicting and controlling history (v. 21).

God's control of history involved a radically new manner of behaving with the defeated enemies. He did not demand harsh payments and slave service. He wanted recognition and worship (vv. 14-15). He offered salvation not only to Israel (v. 17) but to all nations

(v. 22). His ultimate purpose was not victory in war but that all the world should know and bow to the Divine King (v. 23). They should see that only in Yahweh "are victory and strength to be found" (v. 24, TEV; compare NEB).

The prophet added a final note to his argument. Israel had looked forward to their day of military might and supremacy. The prophet said such might belonged only to Yahweh (v. 24). Israel must be content to let God prove that they were in the right (v. 25; see NIV; KJV). God did not call them to boast of their military victories. They could praise and boast only in God's victory of convincing the nations that "there is none besides me" (v. 21).

Bearing Your Burdens (46:1-13)

Legal dispute. God and his prophet had to argue with Israel repeatedly. Exiled Israel had gone so deep in self-pity at the thought of losing their homeland, their Temple, and their political power, that they could not believe that God had any power to save. The prophet turned to bitter sarcasm, picturing the fate of Babylon. It, like Judah, would go into exile. Before it could go, it would have to load up its gods "Bel," the chief god, and his son "Nebo," on donkeys so the deities could join their people in captivity (v. 1). All the Babylonian gods were good for was to burden down the poor beasts. People could not bow down to such gods! Why the gods themselves had to bow down, and donkeys had to bow down under their weight.

Yahweh was just the opposite. He had carried Israel's burden from her birth (v. 3) and would continue to do so (v. 4). He carried what he created, saved what he shaped. No one had to shape him (v. 6) or carry him (v. 7). Unlike any other thing which claimed to be god (v. 5), Yahweh could hear and respond to the burdens of his people (v. 7).

If only Israel would look up from her self-pity, which was her sin of the moment (v. 8), and remember her history with God (vv. 9-10), then she would understand that just as in the past, so in the present and future, "My purpose will stand,/and I will do all that I please" (v. 10, NIV). Yes, even if God pleased to call his ruler from a far eastern country rather than from Israel (v. 11), he would still accomplish his purpose.

Israel must quit being stubborn (v. 12) and get ready for God's great new action in her history. Even though he was using a foreign king, his purpose was for the salvation of his people Israel (v. 13). Would Israel give God the freedom to act out his purposes in his way instead of theirs? Would Israel let God do a new thing? Or was Israel already such an expert on God that she could no longer be surprised by his new plans and actions? Was God trapped in Israel's theology?

Calling the Chaldeans to Complain (47:1-15)

Call to lamentation. God's people spent years in Babylonian captivity complaining of all that had befallen them (see the Book of Lamentations). God turned the tables. He said it was time for the captors to complain. He described precisely how they were to carry out the lamentation rites (vv. 1-3). They would be taken captive.

Power lay not with Babylon but with the Redeemer, the Lord of Hosts, the Holy One of Israel (v. 4). He had decided to avenge his people (v. 3). He had used Babylon for his purpose to punish his people. Now he would use Cyrus to punish Babylon and rescue his people (v. 6). Babylon had become proud and secure, claiming to be the only world power (v. 8), but this was a title which belonged to God alone (for example 45:14).

Babylon thought she had the secret to success. She had developed a complex and comprehensive system of finding the will of the gods through various kinds of priests, prophets, astrologers, diviners, and sorcerers. They thought they could determine the future from the stars, the livers of animals, contact with the dead—almost every way imaginable (v. 9). God brought them up short. They had forgotten the One Way. Despite the great reputation of their various kinds of prophets and of their great, wise counselors, they had to prepare for lamentation and mourning. The God of Israel, not the wise men of Babylon, controlled the destiny of history (vv. 10-11). The divine speech became quite sarcastic (v. 12). Keep on keeping on! Perhaps, you might just succeed (but I know better). The truth is that all their ways of seeking the future had just worn them totally out (v. 13) and given no real help (v. 14). They had no Savior (v. 15).

The word of the prophet was directed to the exiles. They should not be tempted by Babylon's useless systems of predicting the future, no matter how intricate and intriguing they might be. Israel must trust the prophetic word and look for the day of deliverance, the day of new destiny for God's people.

Revelation and Release for the Rebels (48:1-22)

Legal dispute. The prophet argued with his audience who continued to doubt that God could really be acting as the prophet said. He began by identifying his audience as physically descended from Jacob and Judah and known to the world as Israel, the people who made all their international agreements and public proclamations in the name of Yahweh, the God of Israel (v. 1). But the prophet noted, they do not do it "in honesty or sincerity" (NEB). Rather the people glibly recited religious clichés (v. 2). God had been faithful (v. 3), but Israel had not; for she had relied upon idols just like Babylon and the other nations (vv. 4-5). Israel had refused to accept the evidence put forth by God.

Now God would do something new. He had already announced it in their hearing (v. 6) and was now ready for them to see it. The question was whether they would accept it and fulfill their role as witnesses to what God was doing. God stopped to emphasize that what he was about to do was brand new, something never revealed before (vv. 7-8a). This would not have been necessary had Israel been faithful to her calling. But she was not, so God had stored up this new act until now (v. 8b). Israel could not claim to be an expert on God, for he had something new in store (v. 7).

The something new was an act of pure grace. God had not and would not totally destroy his people. This new act continued the purpose which God had always had, that of bringing praise and honor to his great name (v. 9). This was the only reason he had not totally destroyed his people. They could still fulfill this function among the nations, who must not be able to ridicule and mock God and glorify another god instead of him (v. 11).

God thus called Israel to court again (vv. 11-14) and repeated the evidence from creation (v. 13) and from prophecy (v. 14). He then revealed the basic reason why he astounded Israel and used Cyrus: "The Lord loves him" (v. 14). Could anything be more heretical! How could God love an enemy king? Certainly he loved Israel but, of all Israel's kings, only Solomon was said to be loved by Yahweh (2 Sam. 12:24).

The only other individual in the Old Testament said to be loved by God is Cyrus. Israel could hardly believe her ears at such a pronouncement! No wonder they continually debated with the prophet. But the prophet stuck to his word. God loved the Persian king and would use him to fulfill the divine purpose. God had called him (v. 15). For such a startling word, the prophet could only point to his conviction that God had sent him and his Spirit (v. 16).

Again God and his prophet tried to convince the reluctant audience. The new act with Cyrus was not aimed against Israel. It should teach Israel and bring profit to Israel, directing Israel in the way she should go (v. 17). God had intended all along to bless Israel (v. 18; see Gen. 12:1-3), but Israel would not cooperate. Now Israel had one more chance. God gave new marching orders. Out of Babylon! (v. 20). But Israel could not simply march. She was to be God's witness, to bring glory to his name to the ends of the earth (v. 20).

A word of comfort accompanied the word of command. The prophet described how God had helped Israel escape from Egypt (v. 21) and thus set this forth as an example of what would happen should they decide to leave Babylon at his new command. But would Israel quit arguing with God long enough to believe his new word and act upon it?

From all this, a final lesson is drawn, a lesson which is repeated in 57:21. The wicked will not find peace, wholeness, the good and full life. Did Israel belong to this group?

Sending the Servant for Salvation (49:1-6)

Report of commissioning. This is the second of the servant songs (see 42:1-4). The servant of God spoke to the nations in the language often used to describe prophetic calls (compare Jer. 1:5). He acted as if he were an ambassador or messenger from the court of Yahweh to the royal courts of the nations, presenting his credentials. He was God's secret weapon (v. 2), protected by the Lord. God had installed him in the office of the royal servant for the Divine King (v. 3). The last part of verse 3 must have astounded the prophet's audience. The prophetic commissioning narrative was not talking about a single person's experience with God. This testimony was meant to be Israel's witness. Israel, who was pining away in Exile complaining about her fate, was supposed to be presenting her credentials as God's royal representative to the far-off lands. She was supposed to be glorifying God.

As often in prophetic narratives (for example Isa. 6:5,11), the called one complained to God that the task was too great and his power too small (v. 4). The complaint probably echoed the words the prophet heard when he announced God's promises. The exiles saw the whole history of Israel as adding up to nothing, literally to chaos. They could only resign themselves to the fact "yet in truth my cause is with the Lord/and my reward [or compensation] is in God's hands" (NEB, v. 4). As usual, God had an answer to the complaint (vv. 5-6).

God had sought to use the servant to bring Israel back to him. What? How could servant Israel bring Israel back to him? The prophet used mysterious language to arouse his audience's curiosity. He also implied a scandalous theology. Maintaining the personal language of the prophetic call, he said God had used the servant to turn Israel away from her sins. But if the servant was Israel (v. 3), then the prophet has divided Israel into two groups—the servant and the sinner. Here the implications of 48:1-5 are carried forward. Not all Israel was Israel, the people of God. Israel by birth was not Israel of God. Israel the servant had a mission to Israel the sinner. The commission as royal representative of God was not automatic for every Israelite. It came to those willing to quit complaining and to accept the assignment.

Accepting the assignment meant not only bringing glory (42:8,12; 43:7; 48:11) to Yahweh but also to receive glory and strength from him (v. 5). The Divine King shared his power and glory with his royal servant.

The astonishing element of the servant's commission remained to be revealed. The Exile had not narrowed the scope of servant Israel's commission. Rather it presented opportunity for widening that scope. It should have been evident in Exile that the major task of servant Israel was to revive Israel, but this was "too light a thing" (v. 6) for God's servant. He needed new responsibilities. What a shock when the prophet revealed what the new responsibilities meant!

Israel was to be a light to the nations (v. 6). She was to get out of her mourning clothes, dress in royal regalia, and present herself as

God's ambassador with full credentials at the foreign courts. The desperate situation of God's people was no cause for complaint but a chance to carry out a calling. God wanted to save the ends of the earth. He had commissioned Israel to be the servant carrying out the commission. Would Israel rise to the task or remain seated in her mourning?

Prosperity for the Prisoners (49:7-26)

Legal dispute. Israel was not satisfied. She continued to argue. God continued to answer through his prophet. It might seem like the impossible dream for an exiled people so reviled and despised to achieve the position described for servant Israel. The Holy One was, however, also the Redeemer, faithful to his promises and purposes. He had chosen Israel. She could not fail (v. 7).

The interpretation of verse 8 is not simple (compare translations). The reading probably should be, "In a favorable time I answered you, and in a day of salvation, I helped you in order to form you and give you for a covenant to the people to establish the land and to give as an inherited possession the decimated inheritance" (AT).

The prophetic proclamation of salvation was God's answer in the day he chose to recreate his people and give them a new task. They could not, however, brag about their covenant relationship with God. Indeed, God had made them a covenant (see 42:6) for the nations so that they could gain God's salvation. Only in this way, could Israel hope to inherit again her land. This was a new style of conquest! Would Israel march obediently to these orders as she had under Joshua?

God's marching orders are spelled out (v. 9). Get out of hiding from the nations and march through the wilderness where God will protect you. Israel included not simply the Babylonian exiles, but the exiles around the world, even in southern Egypt (Syene, v. 12). Along the march, Israel had a hymn to sing (v. 13).

The people could not get caught up in the prophet's exciting good news. They preferred to argue (v. 14). They wanted more than the word of a prophet they had no real reason to trust. They wanted to stick to the facts. God had forsaken his people.

Again, God had the answer. God had more love for his children than the most deeply devoted mother (v. 15). He was the Divine

Architect, who had written the plans for his city on his own hands where he could never lose them (v. 16) The translation of v. 17 is difficult (compare RSV; NIV; NEB; KJV). It is a word of assurance that the city will be rebuilt without difficulty. The word "builders" (v. 17) includes a play on the word "sons," which is spelled quite similarly. This is then taken up (v. 18) to describe the returning exiles forming the jewelry which adorns Zion's bridal gown.

God's promise included a renewal of the promise of a rapid population growth for Jerusalem, which totally surprised the bereaved mother city (vv. 19-21). The nations would become the beasts of burden bringing the population back to Jerusalem. The rulers of the earth would again pay homage to Jerusalem (v. 22). All of this was to reintroduce Israel to her God (v. 23). The lesson to be learned is spelled out in proverbial style (v. 23b).

The persistent people continued their argument (v. 24). God patiently answered (vv. 25-26), for he had a purpose in what he was doing. He wanted the entire world to see what he did for Israel and thus come to truly know him (v. 26). Yes, God put up with the pitiful complaints of his people to perfect his plan. He wanted to reveal his person and his nature not just to Israel, but to the whole world. Israel was content to continue her queries.

Examining the Exiles (50:1-3)

Courtroom trial. God found himself once more placed as the defendant in a trial. He came out questioning Israel. He used Israelite family law to defend himself. If he had divorced his wife Israel, he would have given her a "bill of divorce" and could not remarry her, since she was now married to Babylon or the gods of Babylon (compare Deut. 24:1-4). If he sold his children into slavery to pay his debts, he would have no further claims on them (compare Ex. 21:7-11; 2 Kings 4:1). Yahweh denied both charges. Israel, not Yahweh, was the guilty party and deserved the fate she received; but she still belonged legally to Yahweh, for she had no divorce certificate nor any bill of sale.

Yahweh then looked at the court and asked where his accusers were (v. 2). There is included here a wordplay on customs of hospitality. Yahweh came, but no one welcomed him at the door.

Was he an unexpected guest? Had his own people not learned from their history that he was their Redeemer and deliverer, as shown by his Exodus miracles? God was at the door to bring an end to the captivity of his people. The darkness of nature was a symbol of the mourning because of the captivity. However, the people did not see God's sadness nor his readiness to deliver them. God's people continued their mourning and their accusing God of inactivity on their behalf (v. 3).

The Servant's Sermon (50:4-11)

Prophetic song of confidence. (Compare Pss. 4; 11; 16; 23; 27; 62; 125; 131.) This is the third of the "servant songs" (see 42:1-4). The servant again spoke in first person (see 49:1-6). In contrast to the complaints of his audience, he testified to his trust in God despite all the persecution and mocking he had faced (v. 6). He was confident because he had found his God-given mission. The servant had a word of comfort for his tired, complaining companions. He had such a word because each morning he listened to his God for a new word (vv. 4-5).

Such communion with God led to confidence even in the most difficult situations (v. 7). He could be taken into court in the land (v. 8), but his attorney would vindicate him. No judge could possibly pronounce him guilty (v. 9). The servant's Babylonian accusers stood helpless. They would gradually wear out or gradually be destroyed like a good suit of clothes, but his God sustained him (v. 9).

Suddenly, the servant changed his tune and faced his audience. He confronted them with *the* question (v. 10). The test of being on God's side, as was the servant, was obeying the voice of the servant commissioned by God. The servant, like the rest of the exiles, had no special light that showed him the way. He had simple trust in God day by day, morning by morning (v. 10; compare v. 4).

The prophet was fully aware that not all Israel fit the description of fearers of Yahweh. He turned to this group and pronounced the sentence upon them. They would be caught in their own firetrap (v. 11). (Note that the precise translation of verse 11 is difficult. Several translations should be compared.)

Look and Listen to the Lord (51:1-23)

Legal dispute. The people continued pouting and pleading with God. They had a simple case: We are pious people, direct descendants of Abraham and Sarah, but so few in number and helpless. God had a direct answer: Look at the meaning of your family tree rather than its many branches. God started with only Abraham and Sarah and that when it seemed impossible for more to come. If the hallowed ancestors could accept God's promise and begin his work with the nations, how much more should you believe the new message of hope? God will indeed comfort Zion (v. 3).

God commanded his people to quit listening to their own feeble frustrations and give heed to his new edict. The Divine King had proclaimed through the world that his time of salvation for his people had arrived (vv. 4-5). This salvation would be unlike any previous deliverance from enemies which Israel experienced from her God. It would include all nations. Indeed, the nations were waiting hopefully for the new day (v. 5). It would include all time, even after the natural order had gradually eroded away (v. 6).

Still the people grumbled (v. 7). They knew the law of God and kept it, but it did not help their situation. They remained the object of mockery and jokes from their captors (v. 7). God reminded them of his previous promise. Such men would die, but God's promised salvation was eternal (v. 8).

The people simply responded with a traditional lamentation. They tried to wake God up (vv. 9-10; compare Pss. 44; 80). He had talked so much about creation and Exodus proving his power. They asked, Was it really you who did all this? For Rahab (v. 9), see 30:7. The prophet answered with a verse of a hymn (v. 11; compare 35:10). Then he introduced an oracle of salvation (vv. 12-16). There is no reason to fear, for God comforts you (v. 12). The comfort is not pie in the sky. It makes sense. The people you fear are simply mortals who will die. Contrast them to the eternal Creator, whom you seem to have forgotten in your great concern over these mighty mortals (v. 13).

The people retorted: But we are bowed down in slave labor, because the Babylonians are so angry at us. God answered: The oppressors, not you, are going to die. I am setting you free (v. 14). You are safe in the palm of the hand that laid the foundations of the world (v. 16). God acknowledged the situation of the people and confessed that he had been the cause. He had left her totally without leadership politically (v. 18) and religiously (v. 19). God had the answer. He would turn the tables (vv. 21-23). Israel's captors would have to drink the cup which God had first given to Israel!

Zealous for Zion (52:1-12)

Marching orders. The prophet became a commander ordering his troops into action. First, he had to wake them up and get them in parade uniforms ready for the great festival procession. God's people could junk their mourning suits forever and put on their sabbath-go-to-meeting clothes. On this holy day they must march to the Holy City. No longer would they be bothered with the torments of their unclean, uncircumcised captors. They could rise from mourning and free themselves from the captive chains. They were on their way. (Note various translations of verses 1 and 2, for several text difficulties are present here.)

The reason for the command appears in verses 3 through 6. God was going to redeem his people, but not ransom them. He got nothing for them when he gave them to Babylon and would give nothing in exchange now that he was about to redeem them from captivity (compare 43:3).

God then gave a brief résumé of the history of Israel's oppression. It began in Egypt (see Ex. 1—15) and had its climax in Assyria (see Isa. 7—8). The translation and especially the interpretation of verses 5 and 6 are difficult. God promised that he would not let his name be defiled by his enemies but would restore his people and their worship, his people again paying attention to his voice.

For such a joyous, festive return march, the prophet provided the proper hymn (vv. 7-10). This praised the messenger who announced the good news that God had again shown that he was the Divine King of the universe (compare Pss. 47; 93; 95—99). The chorus increased as the watchmen took up the song and watched the Lord parade in royal procession into his Holy City (v. 8). Finally, all the destroyed ruins of the city were included in the mighty choir celebrating the fulfillment of Yahweh's mission for his people (compare 40:1). The climax of the hymn turns beyond Israel again to the nations. God worked among his people to bring hope to the world (v. 10). Yet even the word of salvation had an undertone of threat, for the holy arm of God brought judgment to those who stood against him.

Finally, the words came for which Israel had waited the many years in Babylon, the orders to march forth from captivity (v. 11). The marching orders had specific conditions. They must go as the holy people of God, touching and carrying nothing but the Temple vessels of worship which the Babylonians had taken into captivity as booty of battle (see 2 Kings 25:13-17). God promised Israel time to collect all her holy treasures. They were to march in orderly ranks from captivity. They would not be escapees, fleeing for their lives. They would be the army of God, who would march protectively at the rear (v. 12).

God had given the marching dress, the marching hymn, and the marching order. The only question that remained was who would join in. History proved that the people of the captivity were slow to accept the divine invitation to leave the security of Babylon and march into a new day in the city they would have to restore.

Satisfaction for the Suffering Servant (52:13 to 53:12)

Testimony service. The fourth and final servant song (see 42:1-4) presents a service of testimony in which both God and the congregation lend their voices to the praise of the servant of Yahweh. This may be the best-known text in the Old Testament. It is in many ways the most difficult to translate, interpret, and understand.

Most often students seek to name the person the prophet had in mind as he talked of the servant. The question has been asked at least from the time of Philip and the Ethiopian eunuch (Acts 8:31-34). At least fifteen biblical characters, including Moses, Job, Jeremiah, Cyrus, Zerubbabel, Sheshbazzar, and the prophet himself, have been suggested, along with collective interpretations referring to Israel or a faithful remnant within Israel. To begin with the question and its answer, however, is to miss the thrill of listening to the Word of God and letting it speak a new word to us. The task is much more to seek the message which the prophet sought to bring to his audience with his poem and to see how that message can continue to speak to us in light of our experiences with God.

To begin the study, the student should use as many translations as possible, particular attention being given to 52:14-15; 53:7-11.

God opened the service by predicting the fortune of his servant. Fame and fortune should come his way. He contrasted this (v. 14) with the expectation of the multitudes who were totally horrified at the physical appearance of the servant. The servant no longer looked like a human being. Verse 15 begins with a statement which is difficult to understand in the context, the Hebrew apparently reading, "just so he will sprinkle many nations" (AT, see KJV). The earliest Greek translators understood the text to mean "he shall astonish many nations." Normally, we should interpret a line of Hebrew poetry as synonymous with or contrasting to the line which follows. In this case, the following line reads, "kings shall shut their mouths." This still does not tell us if the reaction is positive or negative. Is it a literal comparison or a military metaphor? Are the nations horrified at his physical appearance or are they stunned to silence by the military might which he brings against them? Or has the servant attained such a high position that all other international dignitaries must wait to be spoken to before they can speak (compare Job 29:8-9). As so much of the servant songs, the text is mysteriously ambiguous. The first verses simply set a mood of astonishment and expectation without allowing one to interpret the specific results.

The scene shifted dramatically. A group took center stage to give its testimony. Are these the kings of 52:15 or the audience to whom the prophet normally speaks, the exiles in Babylon? They echoed the note of astonishment—unbelievable (v. 1). They have seen the arm of the Lord revealed to the most unexpected person (people)! Then they turned to describe the event and again surprise us. They did not tell an event at all. They pictured the life of a most unlikely individual. The person grew up in the presence of God without receiving the blessings of God. Instead, he appeared to be cursed, having no physical attributes which would attract a second glance. People would, in fact, have nothing to do with him (v. 3). He was physically sick (RSV note; NIV; TEV). His fellow citizens avoided him and saw no worth of any kind in him.

Now the astonishing revelation! The group must confess: he carried our suffering and bore our pain (v. 4) when we thought God was punishing him (compare the friends of Job). The problem could not be limited to the physical plane of life. The theological was also involved. He suffered because of our sins (v. 5), so that we might get well. What's more (v. 6), every one of us was involved as we went blithely along our own paths like dumb sheep, while God struck down the servant with the load of sin which belonged to all of us. All the while, he endured without a sound (v. 7).

He even had to go to trial and prison (the meanings of v. 8 are probably concrete, KJV and NEB note, rather than abstract as RSV and NIV). Not even one of his generation even bothered to see what was going on. He was totally cut off from humanity, sick unto death. And all because of the sin of my people!

It was even worse. They buried him with the wicked, who do not even get last rites and ceremonies. They even put him out with the rich enemies instead of with our own people. He had done absolutely nothing to deserve such horrible treatment. What can all this mean? What is the purpose of it all? How could it have happened?

Why (v. 10) Yahweh did it! He chose to make him suffer. Note that the Hebrew text of v. 10 is difficult to interpret. It seems to read, "And Yahweh desired his crushing, he made him sick; if his soul would set up a sin offering, he will see seed, he will prolong days, and the desire of Yahweh will prosper in his hand" (AT). The suffering of God's servant was a sin offering when in the Exile with the Temple destroyed there was no chance for such offerings. What he did would help Yahweh's plan come to pass. God's people in Exile thought Yahweh was silent and had forgotten them, but he had been working in his servant! What a revelation!

That revelation was confirmed. Yahweh gave his own word to the congregation yet again (vv. 11-12; see 52:13-15). He acknowledged the suffering of the servant's soul and promised he would see "the light of life" (NIV). He would be satisfied by his knowledge of all that had happened. He would bring justice, the right, to multitudes. He would carry their burdensome sins. He would be numbered among the mighty heroes because he was willing to die among the sinners. Thus God reaffirmed the judgment of the group. The servant was the bearer of sins for the group. They owed their lives to him. And they had never suspected what he was doing.

We have finished, but we have just begun. Here we see as clearly as anywhere in the Bible why it is necessary to try to understand the historical setting in which a passage is first composed. What peoples were present to join in the testimony of amazement? We will probably never know. It may be that the prophet was trying, as so often, to make the Babylonian exiles see how wrong their complaints about God really were, to see that they, who called themselves servants of Yahweh, had simply suffered the fate that God's servants had to expect to suffer. He also showed them that God could use even their suffering for the good of the nation and the world, if they would see the death of the nation of Judah and the suffering of the people in Exile as a suffering for the sins and sicknesses of the world.

Apparently, the prophetic message gained few real followers. It, like the rest of prophecy, was preserved for a new generation which would read and understand and follow. The words challenged each generation to assume the proper office of the servant of Yahweh with the call to carry the sins of the world, even unto death.

Finally, one lonely Galilean took upon himself the image of the Suffering Servant and followed its calling even unto the cross of Golgotha. God, as he had promised the prophet, honored the commitment of his Son and gave him a portion with the great names of history, indeed installing him at the top of the list. Through that one name, Jesus, all the people of the world have been given the chance to unload their sins and find a new way of life. That new way of life continues to be the old one of the servant of Yahweh. The passage which modeled the Master's way must also mold ours.

Build Bedrooms for the Barren (54:1-17)

Oracle of salvation. The prophet used the language of Israel's worship to call the people to trust God's new promises. An opening hymn (vv. 1-3) responded exactly to their laments (compare Lam. 1). Zion had become like a widow without children. The hymn praised God for fulfilling the promise to Abraham (Gen. 13:1-3) again. Israel would have to build an extension to her house to hold the new additions (vv. 2-3).

This meant that an oracle of salvation calling for Israel to "Fear not" was in order (v. 4). The shame of Exile was past history. Zion's husband came to claim her, and he was one with power to do whatever he desired on earth, for he had created both Israel and the earth. Israel had a right to complain. She had been forsaken (vv. 6-7), but that was only for a moment due to God's justified anger (v. 8). Now a new day had dawned. The only comparison that could be made had to go clear back to the days of Noah when God made a new beginning. Then God made a new covenant with all mankind, a covenant which centered in his work establishing peace with his people Israel and using them to be his light to the nations. Such new work of God was based on his "compassion" (contrast the same term in 47:6). It is the deep devotion of a parent for children, which removes all momentary anger.

Because of such deep compassion, God would rebuild the majesty and glory of Jerusalem, reestablishing not only the outward splendor (vv. 11-12) but also the inner stability (vv. 13-14). The emphatic note here is that such restoration would not be followed by another moment of anger. Rather, God would prevent any future enemy from harming his new creation (vv. 15-17). This was the new inheritance (see 47:6; 49:8), not just land but security. This was God's vindication, the same word translated "righteousness" in verse 14 and indicating the right order which God establishes in his world (see 42:6).

Call to the Costless Covenant (55:1-13)

Street vendor's spiel. Having tried the language of the courtroom, the Temple, and the funeral parlor to get his message across, the prophet finally turned to the language of the marketplace to summarize his appeal to his people. God offered the best buy of the day if they would take it. No store ever offered a better sale. Everything was free. The seller wanted no money. He simply wanted the trust and confidence of the buyer in his product. The product itself was not a frill which was not really needed or necessary. Rather it represented the very basic of life itself! The seller guaranteed the full life in all its dimensions. Who could resist such a bargain?

Yet, there was competition. The prophet knew that other salesmen were offering "that which is not bread" (v. 2), yet claiming it was the basic staple of life. He had to call the customers' attention away from such competitors (v. 2*b*). The prophet promised an everlasting covenant (v. 3), a lifetime guarantee. God would give the people in Exile the same promise that he had given David. The covenant with David (2 Sam. 7) had become the subject of doubt and lamentation (Ps. 89:38-51).

The prophet took the opportunity for a new sales pitch. God was renewing the Davidic covenant. He was not limiting it to one man or one office. The entire nation would fulfill the role once given to

David. That role was now interpreted in a shocking manner. David was not simply to conquer the world and bring glory to Israel. David was to be a witness to the nations so that they would follow his command and come to God. Israel in Exile was to become such a witness that even unknown nations would run to her to find the glory of her God (v. 5). Israel was to be a blessing to the universe (see Gen. 12:2-3; 22:17-18; 26:3-4).

The sales pitch took a subtle twist. The salesman called on the customers to do something quite unexpected. Instead of paying him money for their product, they had to "seek [Yahweh]" (v. 6). Was this possible? Normally the expression meant to go to the Temple to worship (see Deut. 12:5; Ps. 9:10; 105:4), but people in Exile had no Temple. The prophets changed this to mean to seek God's way of life, his life-style for his people (Amos 5:4-7,14-15; Isa. 1:12-17).

For the people in Exile, complaining that God had forgotten them and his promises to David, the prophet said to "seek [Yahweh]" had a very simple meaning. Quit your wicked complaining. Quit thinking that Babylon and its gods have won the victory. Repent, turn back to your God. He is ready to forgive and forget, to turn over a brand new page in history. Just realize that God is different from you (v. 8). God makes plans beyond your wildest imaginations. His new plan includes you, if you are willing to fly high with him rather than stooping down in the misery of self-pity and hopelessness.

God's prophetic word promising a new deliverance for his people could be trusted to bear fruit just as certainly as the rains from heaven produce fruit in the ground (vv. 10-11). There was only one condition. The fruit God's word produces was the fruit he plans, that for which he sends his word. People cannot put conditions on God's word and make him act the way they think he ought to. They must be willing to be a part of his plan the way God has described it through the prophetic word! Will you seek God under these conditions?

If you agree to the conditions, then here's the product (v. 12). God's people will escape their Exile and go out in a glorious procession in which even the natural elements take part. All of this will come to pass for one reason. It will make a name (the literal translation of "memorial," v. 13) for God, a sign which can never be erased from history.

Here then is the summary of the message of chapters 40—55. God had planned salvation for his people. He sent his prophet with the word of God to announce this salvation. The people must decide to climb out of the depth of despair to join the journey of joy along the wilderness way to be a witness for the world to the glory of God.

Renewal After Return
56:1 to 66:24

The sad fact of history was that God's people believed the prophecies of salvation just as little as they did the declarations of doom. Cyrus did conquer Babylon in 538 BC and did allow the exiles to return to their homeland (see Ezra 1; 6). Only a small percentage desired to go. They began to rebuild the Temple, but various types of opposition and disorganization stopped the work until Haggai and Zechariah got it started again in 520 BC.

The Temple was finished and dedicated in 515 BC. The prophetic sermons in Isaiah 56—66 deal with the problems of this period of history, as a people sought to gain their identity, encourage their scattered parts to come home to Zion and join in the task set out for them, and to find the life-style which God desired for them in the new historical situation.

Offer Open to the Outcasts (56:1-8)

515 BC, Priestly instruction. The prophet faced the community as it began anew its Temple worship and yet lamented its political situation. He tried to show them what was necessary to be people of God and maintain the hope of the people of God in their situation. The new accomplishment of building the Temple did not mean that salvation had arrived. Rather, salvation was still in the future (v. 1; compare 46:13).

The building of the Temple did not mean that a new way of salvation had been found, that of Temple worship and sacrifice. The first order of business for a people who had built God's house for him to dwell in their midst was to build a life-style suitable for serving in the presence of the holy God (compare 1:17). Such a life-style was separated into two parts (v. 2): religious service and social justice. Sabbath worship had become especially important as a sign of Yahweh's people at the time when they had no Temple. The prophet said such loyalty to God's day must continue when the Temple had been restored. But Sabbath loyalty could not replace righteousness.

Israel consistently argued about the role of foreigners in her worship life (see Deut. 23:2-9; 1 Kings 8:41-43; Ezra 4:1-6; 9:1-5; Neh. 9:2). The prophet spoke the clear word of God carrying out the first steps of the commission of Yahweh's servant to bring justice to the nations (42:1-4). The eunuchs could not experience the blessing of a multitude of sons as promised in 54:1 but would be given a greater blessing, a memorial plate in the Temple which would hold them up as examples for coming generations (vv. 4-5). The foreigners, likewise, would be admitted to the Temple and accepted by God (vv. 6-7). God's purpose was not to exclude but to include (v. 8), and this purpose must not be seen as limited to one period but continued so other outcasts could find the open door to God. But just as with the people of God (v. 1), the new converts must find a new life-style suitable to the presence of God among them (vv. 4,6).

Devouring the Dumb Drunkards (56:9-12)

Prophecy of disaster. The Exile experience did not substantially change Israel's upper class. They refused to learn. They had the commission to be watchmen protecting God's people from outside enemies. Instead, they became the enemy from whom God's people needed protection. They went to sleep on the job (v. 10) and worked only for their own gain rather than to help the people (v. 11). A drinking song was their theme song (v. 12). They had no consciousness that God held them responsible or that God could again come to punish a people who refused to be his people.

The Illusion of Idolatry (57:1-13)

Courtroom trial. The religious condition changed as little as the political. The people tried to cover their bets on all sides by worshiping as many gods as possible, just like all their neighbors. The result: the truly righteous man died without anyone noticing. The people were too busy trying to satisfy the demands of all the gods (v. 1). Peace for the righteous man came to be an escape from the world's calamity into the peace of death (v. 2).

All the while, the majority of mankind were "making sport" of such righteous fools (v. 4). They were enjoying themselves amid the fertility cults which used sexual rites in an attempt to ensure the agricultural and personal fertility of the nation (vv. 5,7-8). They went so far as to sacrifice their own children (v. 5). The exact translation and interpretation of verses 8 and 9 remains unclear, though the reference is certainly to worship of foreign gods. In all of this, the people totally fooled themselves, thinking they had something when all they had was a pure illusion. Only Yahweh, the true God, could give such hope (v. 10).

Having called the sinners to court (v. 3) and listed the accusations against them (vv. 4-10), the prophet asked the people to defend themselves (v. 11). Did they refuse to worship Yahweh because he had been so patient with them and held his peace despite all their sins?

Then the prophet turned with a speech which has a double meaning (v. 12). He would tell the defendants of their right and proper (legal?) actions. He would also describe their "righteousness" in performing all their religious acts. Nothing would help them at this point. The time for sentencing had come. The sentence was simple. God would leave them to the illusion of their idols (v. 13). The sentence was also negative. They would not take part in the new inheritance which God was to give to his people. This was God's judgment on those who were not faithful to him. They did not receive the gifts they thought their idols could give them, and they did not receive the inheritance which God promised his people.

Healing for the Humble (57:14-21)

Promise of salvation. Return from Exile did not remove all the obstacles in the way of the people of God. The prophet had to repeat the call to prepare the way for God's new work of salvation (compare 40:3). God sought to build a path for his people in their own homeland as well as in foreign exile. God remained high and lofty (v. 15; compare 6:1). The high and holy God chose, however, to dwell not only in heavenly isolation but also with the humble (v. 15). He wanted his people to accept the obstacles in their path and continue to trust their God until he had cleared the path for them.

The people continued to complain that God's anger was endless. The divine reply was simple. God was the creator who had given life for men's nostrils (Gen. 2:7). Anger and death could not be his final word. Divine anger had had a justified cause, the coveteousness, the greed of his creatures (v. 17). God had tried to punish and bring his creatures back to himself (v. 17). That had not worked out. Now God would work in a new way. He would heal the guilty ways and thus bring comfort (v. 18; compare 40:1). This would transform the words of mourning into words of praise.

The healing would have an unexpected effect. It would not be limited to the small area around the rebuilt Jerusalem. It would encompass everything far and near, particularly those Jews who had not yet been faithful and returned to Jerusalem from their various places of exile. Still, it was not universal healing. The wicked would face judgment, not peace (vv. 20-21).

Taps for the Transgressors (58:1-14)

Priestly instruction. Again the prophet assumed the role of the priest to tell Israel what was expected in her new day with her new Temple. She thought that she had to carry out precise fasting regulations to show what she was willing to give up in the name of religion. The word of God came with an important announcement. The sin question, not public ritual, was central to religion.

The people continued in their daily religious practices in the Temple, putting on a great show as if they observed the rights and responsibilities which God placed upon them. They even went so far as to complain to God that he was not taking proper notice of all their good righteous acts (v. 3).

The divine answer came clear: Your fasting is none of my business. Indeed, you are the ones who find pleasure in it, not me. You cause others to work all the time for you so that they cannot participate in the worship services. You end up quarreling and fighting when you are supposed to be worshiping (v. 4). God did not seek the precise fulfillment of regulations (v. 5), but the concern and help for other people who were in need (vv. 6-7).

The concrete behavior of helping others, not ritual fasting boosting one's own religious ego, was the key to divine blessing (vv. 8-9). New skin would heal the old scars, while personal right relationships with God and other people would serve as the mediator, bringing the individual to join the divine caravan on the path of life. God's glory (compare ch. 6) would be the rear guard protecting the caravan (compare 52:12). In this condition, the person could call upon God and expect an answer (contrast v. 3). Proper concern for the poor and oppressed (v. 10) would result in divine leadership and blessing (v. 11). This would have national implications, for the rebuilding of Jerusalem and the nation could then continue (v. 12). The good old days would return (v. 14) if proper respect for God and his worship ruled the day (v. 13). The prophetic lesson was complete. Prophetic religion had been defined, a combination of proper conduct in relationship to the world's needy and proper respect for the worship observances which God had set forth, not those that people took personal pleasure in.

Separated from the Savior by Sin (59:1-21)

Service of repentance. The people complained that God had lost the ability to hear and help (compare 50:2). The prophet answered with a resounding No! Sin had separated them from God (v. 2). The sin is then precisely described (vv. 3-8): oppressing the poor (v. 3; see 1:15), corrupting the legal processes (v. 4; see 1:21-23), and scheming and conniving to hurt others in order to pad one's own pockets (vv. 5-7). The latter charge appears in proverbial language like that of Prov. 1:16; Ps. 58:4. Their sin was succinctly summarized in verse 8. They had no knowledge or concern for peace and justice.

The prophet suddenly joined his people in a confession of sins (vv. 9-14a). The people agreed that they could not expect God's just and right order to reign among them (v. 9) when they had sinned in the manner the prophet had described. They described the very essence of their sin. Outwardly it was directed toward the harm of other people and the health of their pocketbooks, but inwardly it was a rejection of God himself (v. 13).

God answered such confession with a promise of salvation (vv. 15b-21). God was angry that his people suffered without anyone able to restore the proper order (vv. 15b-16). So the Divine Warrior equipped himself for battle (vv. 16b-17). His purpose was to maintain his own respect and honor among the nations. Thus God promised to come to his people as their Redeemer (v. 20), but only to those who joined in the confession of sin. His redemption was carefully defined in terms of a covenant promise (v. 21). The prophetic spirit and word would abide with his people forever. Here is salvation, God's people hearing the prophetic word pointing out their sin, joining the prophet in confessing their sin, and hearing the word of divine promise bringing deliverance from their crisis situation. Only on the Day of Pentecost did such a constant abiding Spirit come to the people of God forever!

Gathering Around the Glow of God's Glory (60:1-22)

Promise of salvation. God's people had returned to their city and tried to rebuild it and the Temple, but something was missing. Their hopes and dreams had not been brought to reality. Despair and frustration began to set in. The prophet arose to reassure his people and call them to attention. God was going to act for them. The darkness of despair and defeat would cover the earth, but God would shine his glory upon them (v. 2), so that the light of his glory would attract the nations to Jerusalem (v. 3). The nations would bring the remainder of the exiles back to Jerusalem (v. 4) and would bring rich tribute to rebuild the city in all its glory (vv. 5-14).

Yet the people of Zion must accept one small detail. These foreigners would also come to worship at the Temple, and God would accept them (see 2:2-4; 55:5). The event would, at the same time glorify the people of Zion (v. 9). Zion would never have to shut her gates in fear. Rather she would have to keep them open twenty-four hours a day to accommodate all the traffic bringing her gifts (v. 11). Any nation which did not join in the procession to Zion would be obliterated from the earth (v. 12).

God's marvelous new day of salvation would not be a passing fancy, but would be eternal (v. 15). All would come to pass so that Israel might know Yahweh her God and rest assured that he was her Savior, not her silencer. The day of salvation would be marked by top-quality goods rather than make-do materials (v. 17). The buildings would no longer serve defense purposes. Rather, everything would join in the praises of the Savior (v. 18). Salvation would be so complete that Zion would no longer have to depend upon unpredictable natural phenomena for her weather and light. God's glorious presence would outshine the sun, so that darkness would be no more (vv. 19-20).

Such marvelous new promises are possible only under one condition. The people themselves must be totally different. They are part of the proper order of God's universe, turning totally away from the sins they had confessed in chapter 59. Then they would be able to claim possession of their Promised Land forever, without worry that an enemy might take it away or that God would again punish them for their sins. Under such conditions, the promise to Abraham of many descendants could again be fulfilled. Such promises depend, in the final analysis, not upon human effort, but upon the divine nature (v. 22). God's people will gather for the glorious day when God chooses to reveal his glory among them.

Gladness in God's Garden (61:1-11)

Commissioning report. The prophet described his commissioning by God to minister to the needs of the post-Exilic community (compare 6; 40; 42; 49; 50:4-11). This became the text for Jesus' first sermon in Nazareth in which he identified the role given here as his role (Luke 4:16-21; compare Matt. 11:5; Luke 7:22). The prophetic task centered in preaching to the needy. The content was the action of God to meet their needs (vv. 1-2). The source of the task was the divine Spirit (see 59:21). The time when God would show his favor remained indefinite, but sure (v. 2). The result was that the mourning and complaining of the people in Jerusalem would be stopped once and for all (v. 3). The purpose of the task was to bring glory to God (v. 3). Glory here is not the term usually used in Isaiah (see 60:1), but refers to that which brings praise and pride. The long term results would bring the restoration of the city (v. 4).

The new situation of salvation produced by the prophet's proclamation would bring foreign labor so that God's people could tend to the Lord's work, being the ministers to the nations (v. 6), from whom they would also gain their living. The text of verse 7 is difficult to translate but appears to promise more land than ever in eternal joy rather than the shame they had suffered under the

Babylonians and in the poor circumstances immediately after they returned home.

The prophet added to his promise of salvation a note on God's reasoning (v. 8). God had decided to restore the justice which he loved while doing away with the violence and robbery the people suffered while he was punishing them. God would pay the wages of suffering to his people and sign an eternal contract with them promising them his justice. This would mark them off so that everyone could immediately notice that they were different—they were God's people, enjoying his blessings (v. 9). Again, the indirect result would be glory given to Yahweh.

The prophet reacted to his own message with a hymn of praise at the work God was accomplishing through him (vv. 10-11). God would cause his righteous order and the proclamation of his greatness to spring up as a plant so that all the nations could see it. This was the goal toward which the man of God worked when the Spirit of God anointed him to proclaim good tidings to the poor and afflicted.

The Restless Redeemer (62:1-12)

Promise of salvation. The community continued to complain that God had not fulfilled his promises. Instead he had been silent (v. 1). God responded to his people's poignant plea by promising to act to reestablish her right order and her state of deliverance (v. 1, NEB). Such work would not occur in secret but in view of all the nations and their leaders (v. 2). Jerusalem's reputation would be transformed, for God would rename her. Rather than a heap of ruins at the mercy of the nations, Jerusalem would be the crown adorning God himself and resting for protection in the hand of God (v. 3). Her new name (v. 4) would be My Delight rather than Forsaken and Married rather than Desolate. God would become the husband of Israel and provide fertility for her land. God would be the happiest one of all at the great wedding feast (v. 5).

God repeated his promise with yet another image (vv. 6-9). He would set watchmen to protect the walls of Jerusalem. Whether these are angelic, prophetic, or military, he did not say. They would imitate God in never being silent (compare vv. 1 and 6). Their task would be unique. They should be the private secretary reminding

God of his engagement calendar, so that he would not forget what he had promised to do for Jerusalem (v. 7). Again, the purpose of his work was to bring praise to himself.

God underlined the intensity of his commitment with a solemn oath. Jerusalem would never again be ruled by foreigners who would demand her products and profits as tribute and taxes (vv. 8-9). Instead, her produce would be used in the great worship festivals in the newly-built Temple.

Having sworn his promise, God called the people to action, using the same language he had used earlier for the people in the Exile (vv. 10-12). A new highway must be constructed, but this one would prepare the way for the worship in the Temple. A new signal to the nations would call the kings to recognize what Yahweh had done and bring the proper tribute (see 60:2). Zion would not have to wait any longer for her wages (see 61:8; 40:10). Again, the reward would correspond to a new nature, for the people would be known as the holy people (v. 12). The nations would thus seek them out rather than laughing at how their God had forsaken them (v. 12).

The people of God were thus called to cease their complaints over God's silence and be ready for God to fulfill his promise. Could they wait with praise rather than pouting?

Our Warrior Wreaks His Wrath (63:1-6)

Response to a watchman. Unable to convince his audience in any other way that God was truly going to fulfill his promises, the prophet painted one of the most gruesome pictures in all literature. He took up the role of the lone sentry watching the international border. He spied movement from the southeast.

Hark! Who goes there on the Edomite border? Is one of our hated enemies (see 34:5) attacking? Is that the royal crimson that I see moving in the shadows?

No, don't shoot. It is I who have promised to save you.

Can it be the Divine Warrior? But why are you so red?

I have done to the enemy just what you have claimed I did to you (v. 3). I stomped them to death like I was pressing grapes to make wine. Remember my promise (61:2). I had to do it all alone, but I was able (v. 5). You have nothing more to fear from all your enemies. I am with you to fulfill what I promised.

Petition for Paternal Promises (63:7 to 64:12)

Lament. (Compare Pss. 44; 89.) The prophet not only responded to the cries of his audience with answers from God, he also provided appropriate language for the people to express their frustration and uncertainty to God. This is one of the marvelous elements of biblical prayer so often ignored by the people of God today. The Psalms and other biblical prayers express quite openly and dramatically the depth of anger and frustration which people of God often feel in moments of crisis and tension. The prayer here begins by looking back at what tradition said about God. He had done so much for them. In the Exodus he became their Savior (Ex. 1—15). He went with them himself instead of sending one of his messengers (compare Ex. 33:2). He did everything possible for them because he loved them like a father. He thought they would respond with the same type of loyal love (v. 8).

Israel shattered God's expectation (v. 10). They "grieved his holy Spirit." The verbal form here occurs one other time in the Old Testament, in Psalm 56:5, which can be translated literally, "All the day they found fault with, hurt my word (or my thing)" (AT). The verb implies bringing deep worry and distress through personal hurt or affront. Israel did this to God by rebelling against him, by not responding to the Father's love with a child's obedient affection. God in turn responded by becoming Israel's enemy instead of the Divine Warrior who acted as her Savior.

This caused Israel to stop and take account. Israel thought about her history with God, especially about the central saving event of the Exodus. Israel used it to raise questions about her present. Where was the God of Moses who had divided the sea for them? Where was the Spirit which had given rest to his people even in the midst of the wilderness? Why did God no longer act to bring glory to his name? (v. 14).

Despite the absence of any signs of God's activities in the present, the people still called upon him to act (63:15 to 64:5a). They called upon the compassionate, fatherly love of God, not upon their righteousness. They could not even call upon their membership in the people of God, for their own patriarchal ancestors did not claim them (v. 16). Their only hope was in their history with God and his love.

Perplexity plagued Israel's present. God had been her Redeemer. He had become her enemy. In so doing he had hardened her heart (see ch. 6). Israel had only one alternative. She ran to God with the plea, Why? You are the only God. You control history. You are our Father and Creator. Why did you drive us away from you so that we no longer stand in awe and respect before you? (v. 17). Why did you let us get in the state we are in? So Israel pleaded with God to come back: We have lost all identity, and you have lost your home (vv. 17b-19). We were your holy people. Now we are no different from any one else. Help!

The call for help is phrased in drastic terms. Tear the heavens apart and come down to us (64:1). Show the enemies thy terrible presence.

Meditation on how God used to act and how he might act again led the poet to stand in silent awe for a moment before the unique nature of God (vv. 4-5), who acts for his obedient, expectant people. Such meditation only brought to mind the present state. God was angry at the sin of the people. (The translation and interpretation of verses 2-6 represent one of the most difficult tasks in all the Book of Isaiah, as a look at several translations and commentaries will confirm.) Despite the claim that God had caused his people to sin (63:17), Israel confessed that she had chosen to sin and that no one any longer called on Yahweh's name (vv. 6-7). God had thus withdrawn his presence from his people and let them suffer the consequences of their sins.

Despite all this, God's people could not simply give up. They came back to God, pleading for his fatherly compassion (v. 8). Could the Creator forget his creature? Could he be eternally angry? Did God know how to forgive and forget? The people described the condition of God's land to him, becoming especially pitiful and poignant as they pictured the ruins of his beautiful dwelling place (v. 11). Could God keep silence forever?

The people thus had a prayer given them by the prophet to appeal to the Father's love and the Creator's pride as well as to confess their own sin and faithlessness. Now what would happen? Would the people be faithful to pray to God and truly acknowledge their condition before him? Would God answer?

Ready Reply for the Remnant (65:1-25)

Promise of salvation and judgment. God had a reply ready for the prayer of his people, but it was not exactly what one might have predicted. He did not simply say, Yes, your Father loves you. What can I do for you, my child? Instead, he drew back in a rather scolding tone and asked, Where have you been all this time? I have been waiting for you to call (v. 1). You were too busy with all your other gods (vv. 2-7), worshiping at their altars and participating in such practices as seeking prophetic oracles from the dead (v. 4a), or eating types of sacrifices forbidden in Israel (4b). "Abominable things" is a general term used elsewhere in Leviticus 7:18; 19:7; and Ezekiel 4:14. Here it includes all other types of sacrifices made to pagan gods.

Such people claimed a peculiar holiness which made them either better than other people or unable to associate with other people for fear the holy ones would be contaminated, or would somehow bring contamination upon God (see Lev. 21:6), or would bring holiness upon other people which would endanger those people's lives (see Ezek. 44:19). God judged such worshipers, making them a continual burnt offering to himself (5b). He did this on the basis of written prophecies (v. 6), probably referring to 62:1 and 59:18. The new generation had repeated the sins of the fathers and had not prayed as the prophet suggested. They faced renewed punishment.

Judgment was not God's final word. He had not decided to destroy them all (v. 8). Just like a farmer decides to keep a bad lot of grapes because a little bit of juice is found which can be a blessing, that is, can provide income, so God had found some reason for hope in Israel. He renewed the promise to Abraham (v. 9), reaffirming that they were his chosen people who would regain the inheritance of the land first given by Moses and Joshua. They would possess both the western valley, "Sharon" and the eastern "Valley of Achor" (v. 10).

A great distinction had to be made. The early prophets had

pronounced judgment on the entire nation. After the Exile things would change. Salvation was promised the servants who still produced blessing, while judgment was brought down upon those who rebelled against God. The individual choice became much more important among a people who had no political power as a unifying force. Judgment came because the people left the Temple to worship pagan gods of "Fortune" and "Destiny" (v. 11). Doom was their destiny (v. 12).

God then pronounced blessings on the righteous and curses on the guilty (vv. 13-15; compare Deut. 27—28), climaxing in destruction of the guilty, but the gift of a new name for the righteous. The other side of the picture was that human blessings and curses could be made only in the name of Yahweh, because worship of all other gods would have disappeared from the land (v. 16). God had indeed forgotten the past troubles.

The new condition of salvation for a portion of God's people could occur because God had done something entirely new (v. 17). The new creation would differ greatly from the old one, being dominated by joy instead of mourning and sadness. The joy would be shared by the people and God (v. 18). The injustices of life would disappear (v. 20). Long life would be the rule for God's people, death at one hundred being like an infant's death which could only be explained as the death of a sinner. All of God's people would live to a ripe old age and enjoy the fruits of their life (vv. 21-23). Every pregnancy would be blessed.

But how could all this come to pass for such a people as the prophet faced? God had an answer ready even before they called (compare v. 1). If God's people would only hurry up and pray! When they did, paradise could be restored (v. 25; compared 11:6-9). Many things are possible when God's people get rid of their gripes and turn to the Lord in honest prayer!

Righteous Ritual Renewed (66:1-4)

Prophecy of disaster. The post-Exilic community came to attach too much importance to the Temple. They thought it assured instant success and power in and of itself. They thus interpreted the prophecies of Haggai and of Isaiah 61 too one-sidedly and demanded that God fulfill his promises immediately, no matter the attitude of the people. God had another word. He took up the language they themselves had used in worship to remind them that God was the heavenly Father who was not dependent upon human beings for anything. He did not need a place to sleep. Anything which they built was simply a part of his creation. If they wanted to do something which really deserved divine attention, then they must fulfill the demands of prophetic religion (v. 2). One important element of that religion underlined here is the close attention to the divine word, the emphasis being on the prophetic promise which the people continued to doubt and the prophetic warnings which they ignored.

The grammar of verses 3 and 4 is not at all clear. The original text does not have "is like" in any of the verses. Apparently the prophet charged the people who were so pleased with their Temple building with ignoring the guidelines which God had set down for worship in that Temple. They practiced both proper sacrificial rites—the first of each pair—and rites of sacrifice which were identified with the worship of pagan gods—the second of each pair. They had chosen their way, not God's way. God would then make his choice (v. 4).

Rendering Righteous Recompense (66:5-6)

Oracle of salvation. The post-Exilic community in Jerusalem quickly became split into camps, as has so often happened in the history of the people of God. One camp began charging the other with all sorts of sins and plots. Apparently one group refused to accept the other as part of the people of God and so "thrust them out" (v. 5, AT). The center of contention, as so often, was the prophetic word, particularly the words of 60:1; 55:12; and 61:6-7,10. The group condemned by the prophet apparently had lost faith that any such grand predictions had any hope of fulfillment, while the faithful few clung to their faith in God's word. The prophet assured his followers that the "brethren" would be embarrassed beyond measure. Indeed, he called his followers to listen for the sound of battle which would show that the announcement of God's payday had been made in the Temple (v. 6).

Birth Brings Bounty (66:7-16)

Promise of salvation. The prophet graphically described the salvation he expected and why he expected it. The rapid increase in the population of Jerusalem brought the birth imagery to mind. Such a population explosion was unique, almost unbelievable (v. 8). If God had brought this to pass, would he stop there? (v. 9). There could be only one logical response: Join in the great birthday celebration. Become part of the family. Let Jerusalem satisfy your needs. Here the prophet implicitly called the feuding parties (v. 5) to reconcile their differences. He called all of Jerusalem to forget their complaining to God and rejoice in what he was planning for Jerusalem. The promises of chapter 61 would certainly come to pass (v. 12). Jerusalem would be able to nourish and raise her multitude of children. Israel would be comforted (v. 13). The claim that God was silent and had deserted his servants (see 64:12) would no longer be raised (v. 14). God would truly come to judge his enemies (vv. 15-16).

The prophet had spoken. Would his new word reconcile the bickering parties in Jerusalem? Or would it simply fan the fire, giving new hopes to one and new reasons to the other to mock and laugh at the foolish hopes raised by the prophet?

Sanctifying Servants for the Savior (66:17-24)

Promise of salvation. The book ends with what we might call a prophetic sandwich. Between two pronouncements of judgment on those who rebelled against Yahweh (vv. 17,24), the prophet painted a glorious picture of God's salvation (vv. 18-23). Judgment would come on those who participated in worship of other gods (v. 17). Special attention is paid to a prominent leader of such worship, though we know nothing else about such a person.

Such abominable worship brought forth the divine decision to reveal his glory once and for all (v. 18). Again, Yahweh planned to act for the entire universe, not just a small portion of it. God would send the survivors of his people to gather the nations to see his sign. The list of nations mentioned only the most exotic lands on the edges of the known world (v. 19). Put may be Libya or another section of

Africa. Lud may also be in Africa or possibly refer to Lydia. Tubal is in Asia Minor southeast of the Black Sea. Javan refers to the Greeks from Ionia. No one was to be excluded in God's attempt to let all the world know his glory.

The mission to the nations would have immediate results. The nations would return the Israelites still in Exile to their homeland. This would represent the acceptable sacrifice to the foreign nations (compare 60:6-7). But God had something more radical. The foreigners who came would not just deliver the remaining exiles and go back home. Some of the foreigners would become priests and Levites, serving in the Temple itself (compare 61:5-6). Native Israelites had no more privileges which they could proudly hold to themselves as their rights from God. God would finally achieve his purpose of extending the light to the nations.

This is the new creation of God (v. 23). The descendants of all the foreign nations can remain people of God participating not just in one unique service of worship but in the regular weekly sabbath worship services in the Temple. This was the prophetic dream, a challenge to the complacency and racial pride of his people and a continual challenge to the people of God to reach out into all the world with the good tidings of God's comfort for all people (see Matt. 28:18-20).

Such a dream was not separated from reality. It was well aware of the other side of the picture. Not all men would accept God's invitation to gather as part of his people (v. 18). God's people would have to see the horrible results of rebellion against God (v. 24). The rebels would not even receive burial, but would continuously suffer shame as worms ate at their corpses, the fires of the garbage heaps of Jerusalem burned them, and they became a symbol of God's judgment upon the wicked (compare Jer. 7:30 to 8:3; Mark 9:48).

Interestingly, the early Jewish community did not like the horrible note on which the book ended and so directed that in worship when the book was read, 66:23 should be repeated after 66:24. Ever since, people have sought ways to avoid the biblical message of judgment, but the biblical word continues to remind God's people that God's promises contain two sides, salvation for the faithful and condemnation for the rebels.

Summary

The Book of Isaiah speaks to us through its great themes—trust, holiness, political and religious allegiance, justice and righteousness, and hope. However, we must realize that the structure of the book provided a message in itself to those who had experienced all the long history through which the book sought to lead Israel. Having seen the fall and rebirth of a people, what was the nation Israel centered in the rebuilt Jerusalem to expect in her relationship with God? What did.God expect from her? The remarkable summary in chapter 1 shows us that the basic message of the book was a call to accept the judgment of God on the fallen city as justified, to repent from the sins which had caused that fall, and to look forward expectantly to God's new day of salvation in their city. The first twelve chapters spell out this theme of restoration through repentance and provide a song for the people to sing as they celebrate God's new day of salvation for them.

Chapters 13 to 23 list the nations God would punish as he worked to bring salvation to his people. The list shocked God's people, for they found themselves on the list. Still, looking back, they could rest assured that just as God had brought judgment upon many of these nations, so he would complete his word of promise and bring judgment on the others. Could the community which had joined the nations in suffering God's judgment wait in expectant trust as God completed his task?

Chapters 24 to 27 took up the language of apocalyptic to announce that God's new work in the history of his people would cover the entire universe. No class of people, no geographical location, no political power could escape. Everyone would be included. While the people of God waited for the great event, they should occupy themselves with two responses. They should prepare the great hymn of thanksgiving which God had provided for them to sing at the appropriate moment, but not before, and they should rid themselves of evil practices which had brought forth God's judgment and which could not be tolerated in the day of salvation.

Chapters 28 to 39 showed Israel that her own military might and that of her allies did not supply the final answer. God could bring victory in the midst of great chaos and overwhelming odds. However, God demanded absolute trust in the prophetic word, not in that of foreign ambassadors. God's people must not seek individual security for the moment but permanent security in the word of God for his people forever.

Chapters 40-55 brought a call of comfort to those who had suffered, but the call was also to trust in the comfort. Israel must forget past complaints and must forsake present complacency to join in God's day of salvation, a day led by the divine servant who suffers for his people. Israel must identify herself and her history with that of the servant and become an instrument of God's salvation for the world. Only then would they be part of God's covenant people.

Chapters 56-66 bring the book to a close with a renewed definition of God's salvation. Divine salvation could not be limited to one people or one place. It was for all who would help the needy, providing justice for society, and would worship God properly in his Temple. People from all nations could be involved. They all could also be involved in God's judgment upon the people who refused to meet God's call for trust. The matter came down to a call to confession of sin and to thanksgiving for what God had done and was doing for his people. God had committed himself to do his part. Would his people respond faithfully and do their part, or would they choose to hide behind the protective walls of the Temple, avoid contact with all other peoples, and complain that God had not fulfilled his promises?

The people of Israel had a history of a long prophetic proclamation. They had the history that stretched even further back to the moment of God's great redemption in the wilderness when he had proved his power to save his people from foreign exile. They had the witness of history that stretched even further back to the creation when God proved that all earth and all history and its origin, its history, had its hope in him and in no one else. Still Israel hesitated to heed God's word, to believe God's hope, to trust God's promise.

We in the history of the Christian church have seen God's history with his people stretch even further. We have seen the promised Messiah come and fulfill the divine promises to his people. We have seen that divine word reach out to encompass the nations of the universe. Yet, still we wait in our churches, much like Israel behind the walls of the second Temple. We know the Messiah who took the role of the Suffering Servant, accepted the commission of the prophet (see ch. 61), and sent his followers forth with an even more challenging and comprehensive commission (Matt. 28:19-20). How do we react to such a greater reason for hope and trust? Is our reaction any different from that of Isaiah's reluctant readers?